DEDICATION

To
My mother, Verbena Gibson,
my wife, Marie,
my children, all of them,
and to
God, through His Son,
Jesus Christ

CONTENTS

FOREWORD

Ted Jefferson was born running. And he's still running today. For 40 years he was on the run from the law. And for the same 40 years, he was on the run from God.

Finally, the law caught up with Ted. And shortly after, in a miraculous moment of grace and love, so did the Lord. Now Ted runs for God.

Ted today is living confirmation that the age of miracles is not over. His conversion, present-day life and ministry are proof positive of the power of the Holy Spirit in the life of a man totally committed to Jesus Christ.

Ted Jefferson was born in a log cabin on a small farm near Eau Clair in northern Wisconsin. Ted's father abandoned his family while Ted was still a little child, forcing his Christian mother to move her family to the slums of Milwaukee where she raised her children in desperate poverty.

Ted grew up angry, bitter, hurt and confused, believing life had dealt with him unfairly. Quickly learning the survival tactics of the ghetto, he launched himself early on a life of mugging, purse snatching, boosting, lying and cheating. Self-hate and condemnation soon drove him into drug addiction and alcoholism, habits he was forced to sustain through robberies and burglaries.

His life of crime and sin was climaxed when one night—his senses inflamed with booze and dope and his mind crazed by fear, anger and hate—he sent three bullets thudding into the body of a friend.

Then God stepped in and forever changed Ted Jefferson from one bad dude into a compassionate Christian filled with love and concern for his fellowmen and dedicated to the ministry of God's Word. Within the pages of this book is a message of hope and release for those men and women incarcerated in prisons throughout the world, for those who are helplessly enslaved to alcohol and drugs and for the parents, spouses and families of those who love and pray for them.

Chaplain Ray Hoekstra
Dallas, Texas

PREFACE

As I lay in my bed in the hospital at the Minnesota State Prison, Stillwater, I looked out the window at the branches on the trees gently swaying in the wind. Everything was so beautiful, peaceful and quiet. And I thought, "How beautiful God has created this world."

Then I thought of how man has destroyed that beauty. Not only the beauty of the land, but the way he has destroyed the relationships with one another that God intended us to have. As I looked around me, I became aware of the misery, pain and loneliness of my fellow convicts. And again I thought, "Why do we punish ourselves? Why can't we accept God as He really is? Why can't we love one another as God wants us to?"

The thought now came to me, "Man has the knowledge to send men to the moon, rockets to planets in outer space. It is truly a pity that man with all his knowledge and wisdom cannot teach men to really love one another."

Black power, white power, red power, hatred, prejudices, riots, bombings, lynchings, heroin, wine, prison, death and finally hell. Charles just had his finger amputated from shooting dope under his fingernail with a dirty needle. Lord help us!

I looked back out the window again. A little bird had landed on the branch nearest my window. I thought, "Ted, how lucky you are, God has really set you free, just as free as that little bird perched on the limb of that tree."

Scripture came to my mind: *If the Son therefore shall make you free, ye shall be free indeed* (John 8:36). I then realized, if man is to be set free from the hate and prejudices that so easily possess him, such freedom must come from Jesus Christ. For if we do not have God we cannot truly love, for *God is love* (I John 4:8).

But seek ye first the kingdom of God, and his righteousness; and all these things shall be added unto you (Matthew 6:33).

Theodore Jefferson
Minneapolis, Minnesota

ACKNOWLEDGEMENTS

To God through His Son, Jesus Christ. For without Him I am nothing.

To Mr. and Mrs. Cary Humphries, who came to me while I was in prison, for giving me encouragement and inspiration and for helping my family until I was released.

To Judy Dorn, my caseworker at the prison, who came to my aid. Without her help I doubt seriously if I would have made parole.

To Maurice Nygard, whose spiritual guidance while I was incarcerated at the prison led me to spiritual heights that I never dreamed possible.

To Rev. Louis Walton, Pastor of Trinity Tabernacle, Minneapolis, who visited me in prison and helped me upon my release.

To Chaplain Richard Knowles of the Stillwater State Prison, for his guidance and help in making it possible for Fair Haven to hold meetings at the prison, and also for appointing me to the Chaplaincy Staff.

To all my other friends and all those who have faithfully supported Fair Haven with their prayers and finances.

May God bless you all and my thanks to each of you.

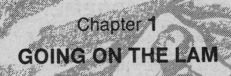

Chapter 1

GOING ON THE LAM

Terrified screams followed
as I emptied my gun
at the man opposite me.

After six days and nights, the high induced by booze and drugs had crested. I was floating without feeling. The present reality of the dingy dive in north Minneapolis was dimly passing before me. Distantly I heard sharp voices, somehow sounding as if they were coming from another room. As these voices argued and cursed, my high became a bad dream—a nightmare.

The haze of the high cleared briefly. My hand felt the cold steel in my pocket and clenched around it. As if in a sequence from some slow motion film, I felt myself rise to my feet.

"No—no, Ted. Don't." someone was shouting.

Ugly oaths crossed my lips and the revolver was out in front of me. As my finger flexed around the trigger, a sudden explosive burst silenced the curses. Terrified screams followed as I emptied my gun at the man opposite me. Three bullets ripped into his flesh. Blood rushed from the gaping chest and stomach wounds. He twisted, gasped, clutched at his side. A frightened, sick groan escaped his lips, as he staggered outside the after-hours joint and collapsed in the street.

I don't know yet if it was someone talking to me or only a voice within me warning, "He's gonna die, man. You killed him."

Numb from all the chemicals I'd ingested and from the sobering shock of what I'd done, I slumped back in my seat, oblivious to the frantic movement of other people in the joint. A crowd gathered outside on the street to watch a man suffer in his death agony. Then I heard the familiar screech and howl of sirens, and someone was moving me along, telling me to hide the gun. Police streamed into the tippling joint asking for witnesses.

I felt people glancing my way, and as they did so my stomach churned. Yet no one talked—the law of the street has ways of dealing with snitches.

Someone nudged me. "You'd better move, man," he whispered.

Instictively I grabbed a drink trom a table and tossed it down. I desperately needed to stay high. The reality of what I had done was too agonizing. Yet I knew that no amount of drugs or alcohol was going to blot this horror from my mind. From that moment forward I would have to live with the fact that I had committed a murder.

Then I was moving—amid the confusion of shouted questions, wailing sirens and flashing lights—out the door. Alone, I stumbled along toward home where my wife and six children hadn't seen me in nearly a week.

It was Christmas Eve 1969. The family was going to celebrate, and some time ago I'd told Marie, my wife, that I'd help get things ready for the holiday.

Some holiday. A man was dead because of me. I felt like crying out to God to end my life right now. Yet I didn't want to die. I was still young—just 37. But what lay ahead of me now?

I'd already done two stretches in Waupun State Penitentiary in Wisconsin, after graduating from terms in the state reformatory at Green Bay and the industrial school in Waukesha. I was already a three-time loser.

So, with my record, what could I expect from a court? My whole life had been a series of one crime following another, moving from one unsuccessful venture to another, from one woman to another, one bar to another, one drug or alcohol high to another. And I knew murder carried a life sentence.

Sick and horrified, but not remorseful, for I believed

only the weak showed remorse, I reeled home and into bed. Sleep came in spurts of fretful, fitful dozing.

Christmas morning I even tried helping the kids unwrap their presents, pretending not to notice the baleful, worried glances from my wife. She said nothing, but her gaze seemed to cry out, "Ted, you're in trouble again."

Finally, I called Marie aside and told her what I'd done. Her eyes brimmed. "No," she said softly, over and over. "What are you going to do now?"

"I don't know," I said. "I don't know."

I did know, however, that I'd have to leave town, leave my loved ones and become a fugitive again. I'd done a bit of running before; it was almost a way of life.

I looked at my kids with their few gifts. My heart should have gone out to them for what I'd be putting them through. I was letting them down, but it wouldn't be the first time. And I really didn't care. The only thing on my mind was how Ted Jefferson would get away and where he would go.

I sat in front of the television for a while that morning, agitatedly waving off my excited children who wanted to show their daddy what Santa had brought them. Finally, they wandered off hurt and confused.

Then the news came on, and a reporter told of the shooting the night before, saying the police had a warrant out for the arrest of Arnold Jefferson in connection with the crime. "Arnold" was an alias I had used occasionally to avoid detection by law officers in Wisconsin, where I was wanted on several other charges. It wouldn't take long for the police to determine that Ted Jefferson and Arnold Jefferson were one and the same.

There were those back home in Milwaukee who would have shaken their heads and sadly proclaimed, "I told you so." They'd been following my dubious career ever since boyhood when I first began my criminal activity. From petty theft, truancy and fighting, I had progressed to alcoholism, burglary, and smoking and shooting dope.

And now I had added murder to the list.

I jumped up. "I gotta get out of here," I snapped. Taking the gun from its hiding place in the basement, I got ready to leave. Marie asked where I'd be going, but I didn't answer, and she knew me well enough not to argue or protest. Yet I knew she would be praying for me and for the family of the man I'd killed.

In my heart I felt this would be the last I'd ever see of my family. And there was a momentary tug in my guts, yet even that was not enough to make me kiss anybody goodbye.

I cut out for Detroit where I had a connection. It was like old times.

I was on the lam again!

Chapter 2
SURVIVING AGAINST ODDS

I joined Mom and Corrine
in an unending search for fuel.

I was born in a ramshackle log cabin on December 7, 1932, the second child and first son of Theodore and Verbena Jefferson. We lived in rural Butler township, just outside of Eau Claire, Wisconsin.

Ours was one of only two black families in the vicinity. The other was my mother's folks, who farmed and preached in Stanley, Wisconsin, about six miles away.

To say our family was poor would be an understatement. There were chinks in the floor, holes in the roof and cracks between the logs where the wintry blasts would rip through and swirl about the tiny hovel we called home for the first six years of my life.

We shivered in the winter, and our only insulation was manure hauled in from my grandfather's farm and piled against the outside of the shanty. It may have saved us some heat, but come the first spring thaws and our house took on the fragrance of a cow barn, infiltrating our clothes, and even—it seemed to me—influencing the taste of the food we ate. Yet in this home, my mother exalted the Lord above all.

In our extreme poverty, we had nowhere to turn for medical help. If somebody got sick, God was our physician. Once when I was nine months old and Dad was off on one of his infrequent binges, I contracted double pneumonia. Mother was alone with my sister, Corrine, and me in that cabin. We had no telephone, and since we lived off a

dirt path, no auto traffic could reach us. The nearest neighbor was over a half-mile away.

In that drafty cabin, Mom stood by, watching me struggle for every breath. In her anguish she cried, "Lord God, this baby is sick and I can't stand to see him suffer any more. He is Yours, and if You want him, take him now. But if You leave him with me and let him live, I will dedicate his life to You. Either way, he is Yours. He is in Your hands."

Within minutes, my breathing became normal and the fever receded. I was spared, but the quality of our lives did not improve.

Life in those early years was strictly survival, eating only beans or potatoes for long periods—and then maybe we'd eat only once or twice a day. But mother always thanked the Lord for every mouthful.

One neighboring Italian family took pity on us and brought over a box of home-canned goods. We literally tore into those jars, only to discover that in the canning process, something had gone wrong and the food had spoiled. It was especially hard on mother to tell us we couldn't eat this food when there was almost nothing else edible in the house.

The steady diet of potatoes, beans and nothing got to my father and, during my fourth year when a younger sister, Alice, arrived, he left for parts unknown, leaving mother in full command.

We tried staying on in the log cabin, but the house was rotting under our feet. One of the few memories I have of that place is the game I used to play with Corrine. We'd drop pennies through the spaces between the floorboards onto the ground beneath, then dash outside and crawl under the house to see who could be the first to find the coins.

From the time I turned three, I joined Mom and Corrine in an unending search for fuel. Mother was unable to operate saws or axes—indeed we didn't own any—so we burned pine knots. Each day we'd set out with gunny sacks to search for these pine knots in stumps of rotted trees, gouging them out with our hands or kicking them out with our feet. It was a day-to-day struggle for existence.

But this sort of life was too stern for a woman with three pre-school youngsters, so we finally moved in with mother's parents in Stanley. Things didn't improve much there, though we ate better after a fashion. My grandparents were old-time, stomp-down Christians and, before each meal, Grandpa would not only read passages from the Bible, he'd often give little sermons too. And around the table each one of us had to recite a memorized Bible verse. As much as 15 to 20 minutes would pass before we actually got to eat. And by then the food was inevitably cold.

Still, I recall liking the farm, where Grandpa kept a few head of dairy cattle in a decrepit old barn that was little more than a lean-to. It would have been condemned by the Humane Society if they had known about it.

Corrine began school in Eau Claire and was the only black child in her room. It must be said, however, that we never encountered any race prejudice there and never heard my family mention any either. All that would come later when, at the age of six, I moved with the family to Milwaukee to join my mother's sister.

Auntie had a shack in West Allis, behind a foundry where we stayed while mother looked for work. Another black family lived close by, and these children, along with my cousins and me, used to climb the soot hills and slag heaps behind the foundry, getting ourselves good and dirty.

One day a foundry worker hollered to my cousin and me, "Hey, you kids want a drink of Coke?"

"Sure," my cousin shouted, and dashed after the man. I followed him, not even knowing what a Coke was, for until then I had never tasted any kind of soda. I watched my cousin happily take a long swallow, and I copied him. The carbonation made me sneeze and choke, and both the worker and my cousin enjoyed a good laugh at my expense.

In a few months, mother found a room in Milwaukee,

and we moved into a house on Seventh Street. And here, my first encounter with racism occurred when a boy from a mixed marriage shunned me. One morning I asked him if he wanted to play with me, but he turned away and brusquely told me, "Get away from me, you little nigger."

At school too, I felt the sting of discrimination—and sometimes from other blacks. I was treated as white because I wasn't hip to the jive lingo of the black ghetto. Instead of "Hey, what's happenin', baby?" as a greeting to dudes on the street, I would say, "Hi there, you guys."

"You talk like a white man, little nigger," one boy told me.

"What's wrong with this dude, man?" other kids were saying.

Some of the kids picked fights with me, and one day on our way home from school, a group of them packed snow into Corrine's and my snowsuits. When they were done we could hardly move, but somehow we both waddled home, thoroughly chilled.

As a result of that ordeal, I became seriously ill again, and a 104° F fever kept me in bed for three days. Then a neighborhood barber who was also a part-time preacher came to the house, laid his hands on me and prayed for me. Though I wasn't exactly aware of what was happening, I felt the power of God for the first time. I distinctly remember losing that rattling congestion in my chest. I sat up and asked for something to eat.

Sadly, this episode didn't bring me to the Lord. Instead it taught me that, if I was to survive with any dignity in this neighborhood, I'd have to start scrapping. I'd have to learn how to defend myfelf. And if I was going to survive, I'd have to learn quick.

Besides, though only seven years old at the time, I knew I wanted revenge on those boys who'd stuffed our suits with snow. "I ain't never gonna let nobody do that to me again," I told Corrine. Yet I was too scared to do anything about it.

I didn't want to be a coward, but I was outnumbered—and I respected numbers. So I used to come flying home

11

after school every day, hoping to outdistance the bullies who kept after me.

Mom sensed that something was wrong, and she didn't want me being cowardly either. Finally she said, "I'm tired of you running in here every day. You got to stand your ground. You're not supposed to be pushed around. You might live a Christian life, but you don't let people run over you. I'm sick of it."

A day or two later, one of the toughest kids in my age bracket was walking behind me, kicking my feet and trying to trip me. "Hey, Buddy," he said—everybody called me Buddy then—"give me your marbles, man."

I stopped, whirled around and hit him. He went down. I was just as stunned as he was, but I felt a giddy sensation. "I can hit, man," I was saying to myself.

From then on, I wasn't to be messed with. In fact, I became overbearing, a bully myself, relishing combat, looking for fights and issuing challenges to other kids on the block.

Then when I was nine, we moved to Eighth Street, and I attended the Ninth Street School. A new turf, and again I had to prove myself. I did by whipping a 10-year-old tough, and soon I became top dog around the school yard.

But one Sunday, at the urging of my mother, I made a "decision" for Christ. It was a halfhearted decision, more for her sake than mine. Okay, so I was going to be a Christian, but Christianity was for prayer meetings and Sundays only.

I fooled no one with my false profession of faith. I resumed my tough guy attitude on the street, and my former friends—decent kids—no longer wanted to hang around with me. I gravitated toward those who were wise and wily in street survival.

As I was developing street savvy and toughness, I managed to do rather well in school too, and was even skipped a half grade from 5B to 6A.

Mother always prayed that I'd get a good education and break out of the cycle of poverty that seemed to ensnare us. She wanted me to amount to something, both for myself

12

and for the glory of God. She'd occasionally remind me that she'd dedicated me to His service—a reminder that nagged and bugged me, for I was thinking that it might me more profitable to be working for the service of Buddy Jefferson.

The mores of the ghetto dictated that money meant influence and power, and you had to get the money any way you could. Everyone knew The Man wasn't going to go out of his way to help the black people, and you had to survive.

One of the tragedies of ghetto life—perhaps because ghettos exist—is that they exact a twisted morality from young children. Ghetto youngsters need people to look up to and admire and, like kids everywhere, they admire success. But for them, there are no doctors, lawyers, teachers or businessmen with whom they can identify. So their heroes are pimps, gamblers, hustlers, pushers—exactly those people most despised by straight society.

The poor black kid who sees the pimp all dressed up, flashing a role of twenties, driving a new car and flouting the law, just naturally figures that's the life for him. So my heroes were pimps, hustlers, boosters and pushers—the dudes with the $50 shoes, the neat threads, the big cars.

Actually, until I entered Roosevelt Junior High School, I hadn't officially gotten in trouble. In fact, I was feeling pretty cocky and sure of myself.

Being a bit short for my age, I can remember dudes regarding me with a there-goes-that-little-Buddy look. But by now I'd earned their respect as a street fighter, so what they said would come out, "Buddy, how you doin'? Look, you want to come with us?"

And, of course, I did. I was always ready for whatever action there might be, whether it was fighting with some other gang or maybe rolling a couple of drunks for quick money.

For all intents and purposes my formal education stopped in the seventh grade. And in the summer of 1944, I formed an alliance with Alvin and Winston, boys who like myself were victims of broken homes. I met Alvin first

13

when he moved in across the street from us. Shortly after, we fell in with Winston, who had already begun a profitable career boosting—shoplifting. The three of us went to a shopping center on Twelfth Street and boosted small toys from the dime store.

Being home with a mother who always praised the Lord, who prayed regularly and always read the Bible, plus demanding regular church attendance, I knew what we were doing was wrong, and that it was a sin in the sight of God. But like so many kids, I caved in to peer pressure. Satan knows now to get a young boy trapped in his clutches. He can make the world look pretty attractive, especially when you've gotten a taste for material goods.

Maybe part of my problem was how Ma handled me. I wanted a bicycle, but knew we couldn't afford one. Ma would simply dismiss my requests with, "If God wants you to have one, you'll have one."

Perhaps, at the time, a fuller explanation of how God worked would have helped me, for kids don't always understand the ways of the Lord, and to be casually dismissed like that created hostility within me. I can remember thinking to myself, "Then I'll steal a bike. If I don't get caught, must be God wanted me to have one."

There were numerous times I'd use that cop-out to justify my stealing. Then after a time—though I really knew stealing was wrong—I began to think it was not altogether wrong. It was all right for me after all, because that was the only way I was ever going to have anything.

I recalled an old black preacher saying that God wanted His people to prosper. So I would prosper. You better believe I would prosper—even if I had to steal!

Chapter **3**

GROWING UP BAD

Life was filled with
devious adventures.

Many of our early rip-offs happened in the junkyard next door to where we lived. We boosted stuff from the place and sold it to other dealers. Or we'd take something from the back of the yard, bring it around to the front and sell it back to the dealer. If the old lady running the place had ever caught on that we were ripping her off, Ma would have been the first to know.

I can't say stealing didn't bother me—it did for short periods of time. But the act of thievery was exciting. The risks offered challenges; it was fun to try to outwit store owners and detectives.

And all this while I remained active in the church—at mother's insistence. I rarely missed Sunday School. As often as not, mother dould drag my sisters and me to midweek prayer meetings which frequently stretched on well past midnight, as children nodded off to sleep on pallets on the floor. This was no small task for mother, for she had remarried and would, over the next few years, bring five more youngsters into the world.

My experience in the small storefront churches led me to believe absolutely in the power of the Almighty. Say what you will about those simple, semi-literate congregations—they were filled with the Holy Spirit. They had no intellectual hang-ups and therefore accepted without doubt that God performed miracles for the faithful.

But I wouldn't place blanket trust in God. It used to irk

me to hear Ma praising the Lord, when she had only one old battered pair of shoes to wear, and her stockings were always scarred with runs and holes.

I kept a basic respect for her, however, and when she insisted I participate in church, I did, even to the point of memorizing verses, taking part in plays and programs, and helping younger kids with memory work. How she had time to make sure we learned the Scriptures, I'll never know, because her second marriage was already souring.

I was 11 now and rapidly developing a chip on my shoulder. Like many young ghetto kids, I felt I was being punished for my economic and racial status. To get back at the system that kept my people in chains, I would boost from white-owned stores.

It was easy then, and it still is today. After a while, you learn to spot store detectives. And if there are two or three kids, outwitting the detective is a breeze. This is how it works. You split up and move fast. The kid drawing the detective goes suspiciously through the store, but takes nothing. The others grab whatever goods they want and split. Later, outside, they divide with the decoy. Because we always had sweaters and dime store jewelry to give away, we made big hits with the neighborhood girls.

The irony of this time in my life was that I still thought I was a Christian. I knew God was real, but when I'd hit the streets I'd do a complete about-face. Maybe this was because I saw mother going through so much agony from day to day, always falling a little more behind each month. So, while I believed in the power of Jesus at church on Sunday, I stuck to street mores Monday through Sunday.

I was 10 or 11 when I began turning on with pot and codeine as well as liquor. And when I was 11 I got busted for the first time.

That arrest was pretty frightening because we kids heard numerous myths about jail perpetuated by adults who hoped my buddies and I would straighten out if we were scared. Often we were told that if the police brought us to jail they'd put us on whipping machines for hours on end and give us only stale bread and water to eat.

But when we were nabbed for shoplifting and truancy, Alvin, Winston and I were brought to the detention center. And there we found things really were't so bad. We were well fed during our two-day stay, and when we were released to our parents, we were given something of a hero's reception by other kids, who were fascinated by our escapades. So it was then that the kids younger than we began to think that our trio was on its way up.

Life was filled with devious adventures. There was always school to skip, truant officers to ditch and store detectives to fool. And—not of little importance—girls to impress. All the while, Ma continued her praising the Lord and telling me that I was headed for great things in His service.

None of this made any sense to me. Ma found her joy in her trust and belief in her Lord. Yet we were always dirt poor.

At the same time, right around the corner, another friend's mother worked as a prostitute. And she was always dressed fit to kill, while my Mom wore ragged, used clothing. This house around the corner had steaks in the refrigerator while we felt lucky to have beans.

This lady who worked at night occasionally gave us kids money for candy or for the movies. And I'd wonder why my own mother who praised God had so little of anything, when this woman who cared nothing about religion was living so much better than we were.

"Is this the way God wants us to live?" I used to ask Mom. No matter how she answered me, I couldn't accept her explanation, probably because I didn't want to. I just couldn't accept the concept that God wanted me ragged and poor.

I occasionally stayed overnight with my friend around the corner, and when I did I'd watch the drunks phase in and out of the house. Money flowed freely in the gambling games my friend's mother had set up in her living room.

The first time I slept over, his Mom was entertaining some sailors in the next room. From our room, we could hear their drunken laughter and ribald conversations.

After about an hour, my friend, opening the door, said, "Theodore, pretty soon there's gonna be some money falling on the floor."

When the men had either passed out or started getting careless with money—quarters, dimes and nickles—we'd dash into the room and snatch the loose coins. There were nights when we'd grab five or six dollars to split between us.

One day during a round of shoplifting, Winston copped a bullwhip from a downtown dealer. While trying it out in the school playground, he accidently hit a girl in the lip and tore it wide open.

Fearing reprisal, we didn't go to school the next day, but we were caught by our probation officer anyway. This time, he thought we should go before the judge before we got ourselves into more serious trouble.

My friends were sent to the industrial school at Waukesha, but for some reason, the judge stayed my sentence. Perhaps it was my mother's sincere Christian principles that he respected, and he hoped that I might be persuaded to change my behavior. He told Ma that if she could get me out of Milwaukee, I wouldn't have to go to reform school.

She had a friend, an elderly Christian lady who lived alone in Owen, Wisconsin, a small rural town near Stanley. So Ma sent me to Owen. But after all that time in the streets of a big city, lapping up its glitter and excitement, Owen was absolute dullsville for a spunky, street-wise kid.

It wasn't peace and quiet I craved; I wanted excitement and action. Within two weeks I proved too much for the lady and she regretfully, but no doubt thankfully, returned me to the city. I was sent to Waukesha for my first stretch in a penal facility.

My first stay wasn't all that terrible. I was, after all, with my best friends. Still, it was a prison, filled with restrictions and limitations, and when my year was up, I was grateful to get out.

I wasn't about to change, though. Too many kids

wanted to know what it was like at the school, and they'd give me cigarettes or pot or beer just to have me tell them all about it. Inside a week I was back at boosting.

There were other, somewhat more respectable ways to make money too, and I gave these a decent try. The bunch from the neighborhood would put together shoe shine kits and go into white taverns. We used to stage "fights" between each other for the patron's entertainment. The "winner" would get to shine all the shoes in the place and get a good tip besides. This would have to be split with the "loser" later on, but nobody bothered to stop these fights because it was only a couple of "nigger kids" banging each other around.

Sometimes the whites would tell us to dance, and they'd toss us coins. We learned to perform like animals in a circus, and, in a way, I guess there was little difference.

But again, I was too much for my Mom to handle. She sent me to my uncle's farm at Rib Lake, Wisconsin. Here I spent the best two years of my juvenile life and even stayed in school on a fairly regular basis. Away from the ghetto, I found peers interested in things other than smoking pot or ripping off stores.

Still, I managed to exert a bit of influence of my own. Being a city kid, I think some of the others were a bit awed by me and simply went along with my pranks.

I had a friend my age, named Larry, a white kid, and both of us were given .22 rifles. We'd ride the bus five miles to school, but instead of going in, we'd walk back toward home where we'd stashed our rifles. We'd spend the day in the woods, target practicing, shooting birds and squirrels, then walk all the way back to town to catch the bus home.

My uncle never suspected a thing until the school called and told him I wasn't there. I can still hear him arguing, "But I saw him get on the bus this morning and he got off when it came back." His discovery of my activities did not make him happy.

I reached my thirteenth birthday in Rib Lake and had enjoyed the country living and tending to chores there on

21

the farm. If I could have remained there, I might never have gotten into the troubles that always found me in the city.

But Ma had gotten a divorce by now, and she needed me back home, where I promptly began dealing in drugs. Ma's response was that I should get right with God and take a more active interest in church.

Looking back on those days, I am thankful for a Christian mother, but I have to feel as if she pushed a little too hard. During my growing up, it seemed as if I was going to church almost every other night—and the services were lengthy. Ma used to say, "If you love the Lord, you want to serve Him and be in His house." But I loved Ted more than God, and for me any church was too much.

I recall one Sunday afternoon sitting on the steps of the apartment building with Corrine. Most of the neighborhood kids had gone to the movies, but we were't allowed to go. The only times I saw movies were those occasions when I sneaked off.

So Corrine and I sat there grumbling and complaining. "After I'm grown up, I'm never gonna go to no church," she said.

"Me neither. I want no part of it," I spat angrily.

And I meant it!

I also told Corrine if being saved meant living poor and hungry, then it was only for fools. Whitey had plenty of bread, and I was going to get mine as well.

Too, the existence of those poor rundown churches made me mad. I felt that the Church was robbing me of my life. I had no freedom, I thought. I was unable to express myself with my friends. Everything in the neighborhood was cool, man, but the church crowd was hot. So how could a dude be cool if he was always having to go to that old church?

I still believe that well-intentioned people do get priorities mixed up, and, like my dear mother, sometimes turn their youngsters from the Church. I used to see mothers drop $10 in the collection plate when everyone knew their children got only one meal the day before. I knew that I'd never make that kind of mistake, because I wouldn't ever give money to a church.

So as much as anything back then, it was my attitude that landed me in hot water. I got busted again boosting from a jewlery store, and off I went once more to Waukesha.

Still I remained tough, cool. That was all right, I said to myself. At least now there'd be no church, and I'd do some growing and toughening. I was 14 years old.

This time the industrial school proved a harsh eye-opener. My first stay there hadn't revealed the bitter realities of such a place. I could take the loneliness, for it gave me time to think about what I might do when I got out—ways to avoid detection—anything I might do to get back at society. I wanted revenge.

But this time I was horrified at the rampant homosexuality I encountered. Before this stretch, I'd never known of its existence. Now I'd hear or witness homosexual rapes and was always shocked to see attacks and arrangements in the public toilet, right out in the open. Shocking, too, was the apparent lack of concern by the institution's staff and guards.

Fortunately, I never got involved in the homosexual scene. Even though I stole and did other things, I still felt something of a moral sense about some matters.

While at Waukesha, I often thought of my mother. I knew how earnestly she prayed for me. In fact, I thought of praying myself. But I resisted, and instead I used to lie on my cot at night and throw all my bitterness at God and ask Him why these things were happening to me. Receiving no satisfactory answers, I continued drinking wine and smoking pot, both of which were easily available inside the school. Though only 14, I was a confirmed alcoholic, totally dependent on the sustaining of a high.

While the monotony of Waukesha used to get me down, it also kept me on my toes. Fights erupted easily among caged boys with explosive tempers. Emotions got worn and frayed, and even rumors started fights or attacks or riots.

23

My tenure this stretch was 12 months, during which time I avoided formal schooling. They gave me a choice of classes or unloading boxcars, and I opted for the latter. This was really senseless. I though I'd be getting back at society by refusing to go to school. But I should have been forced to attend. Had they insisted, I'd have gone and undoubtedly would have been better off for it.

After a few months I settled into the routine and started boxing in the gym and found I was a natural for the sport. Psychiatrists found me a model prisoner who couldn't handle himself outside the institution. But I didn't need them to tell me that. I knew precisely who and what I was. I knew there was no chance I'd ever go straight, because none of my friends would. Still, I avoided conflicts in Waukesha, partly due to my boxing ability, and I was pretty much left alone.

Lacking firm friendships, I began looking to God to ease my burden. I started praying and occasionally read my Bible. In this way I thought I was staying close to God, though I wouldn't yet live for Him. Rather, I lived for Ted and looked forward to my next release.

Release came, but freedom didn't last long. Within a short time, I was back in Waukesha again. But my third trip to that institution was different from the first two in that both the circumstances getting me there and my attitude about being returned were different.

For, this time, I was sent up for a burglary I did not commit. It may have been the only time I was perhaps unjustifiably arrested. I stress perhaps.

I had been out of Waukesha only three weeks and had gone to a movie with some friends. On our way home, we stopped to look in a jewelry store window. That's all we were doing—looking. But it was a white neighborhood, and a lady saw us and phoned the police, saying that some suspicious-looking guys were lurking in front of the jewelry store.

When the cops came up, we knew they were going to hassle us. While they couldn't prove we had done anything, we had been thinking about it. And if they hadn't

24

come, chances are withing a few seconds somebody would have gotten a brick and smashed the window. We'd have grabbed what we could and split.

But since we'd done nothing, I decided not to run away. However, the dudes I was with took off down the alley. I wasn't going to stand there by myself, so I lit out too. But the police had the area sealed off, and they caught us before we'd gone three blocks.

They looked around the store and found a screen had been loosened—obviously from some earlier burglary attempt, but they blamed us for it and took us to the detention center, where we stayed 10 days. Finally, my parole officer came to see me and, without even asking for an explanation, said, "Ted, you're going back to Waukesha."

"I'm not going back if there's a way out," I said.

Another dude named Lollipop had to go back too, because, like me, he had a long record. So they handcuffed us together and were taking us down the steps of the center to put us in a car headed for Waukesha. One of the escorts stopped before he got to the front door and started talking to a guard.

Lollipop, who was about a foot taller than I, tugged and nodded at me. We eased down to the door and stood there a few seconds, pretending to be rapping, relaxing. Suddenly, Lollipop turned and wham—we hit the door and started running down the street.

Because of his great height advantage, Lollipop was half-dragging me behind him, taking two steps to my three. We were hugging and yanking at each other, trying to synchronize our steps as we ran, and it was all but impossible. It was almost as if we were fighting each other.

As we were running, we came to a temporary "no parking" sign that had been placed on the sidewalk. Like something out of a Laurel and Hardy film, we did the obvious. Lollipop went around one side of the sign, and I the other. The sign caught in the handcuffs and we were running with it, dragging it behind, as it clanked along the concrete, sending up sparks as we ran. Onlookers with open mouths gaped as Lollipop and I, clanking sign and all, rushed by.

Just before we heard the sirens and squeals of tires and police motorcycles, we managed to free the sign from our wrists and beat it onto a street only three blocks from where I lived.

On this street were large brick garbage receptacles with iron doors. We had momentarily ditched the pursuing officers, so we took a chance and dashed into one of the bins. It really smelled bad, but we reckoned we could take that for a while. I felt we could get away after dark to my uncle's garage and cut the cuffs off there.

Meanwhile, we thought we were home free. But then the lady in the house decided it was time to let her German Shepherd out. And when she did, he came to the bin where he sniffed us and began barking and snarling.

"Go away, dog," Lollipop whispered, which made the dog all the angrier. He jumped at the bin and tried to get at us. And he kept it up until the lady figured out someone was inside her bin. Then she hailed the police.

By this time, of course, a good crowd had gathered out front. And finally, when things quieted down a bit, an officer kicked at the door. "Okay, the dog's inside. You guys can come out now." I felt pretty small crawling out of the garbage dump and being recoginzed by all the people from my neighborhood.

But that episode wasn't to be my last escape. I was determined I wouldn't stay in any institution again. So I was already figuring out how I'd bust out of Waukesha.

By now I was an old hand at the school. All the dudes knew me, and so did the administration and guards. While things weren't all that bad, I knew I wanted out. I felt caged and couldn't take it any more.

I was thinking escape, and decided it wouldn't be all that hard, either. Especially from the honor cottage. That was the cottage up on the hill where the model prisoners were allowed to live. It was different from the others in that the doors were never locked, and inmates there had a bit more freedom of movement.

I'd never cared before whether I was a good inmate or not, but now I really wanted to be. I wanted to get residence in that honor cottage. And to achieve that, I had to get good work reports, receive no discipline tickets and convince authorities that this time I meant to straighten out. I managed to do this and, within a few short months, received my transfer to the honor cottage.

I bided my time, my confidence building all the while. I knew that people had just walked away before, and a few actually had made it outside. I would be one of the lucky ones. I was sure of it.

Actually, I was in no real hurry to break away, because life was almost pleasant. The honor cottage had a game room, television and lounge, almost like a dormitory at a college. I liked that for a change after living with other tough dudes. I made friends easily and saw that a few of them even looked up to me. That would help too, since I didn't want to split alone.

Evenings I used to talk with a couple of other dudes about running. One was another black name Bullhead, and the other an Indian we called Chip, because he was a Chippewa. I convinced them we could run and get away with it, if we got up early—an hour or so before breakfast.

Now remember, we were still just kids 15-16 years old. And we certainly lacked good sense. We were all set to run, but never stopped to think of where we'd go. Every other escapee used to skip back to his mama's or his girl friend's place, and sure enough the cops would be there waiting for him, and back he'd come. I guess that's where we were headed too, not thinking they'd have us back in no time.

The Waukesha institution is right on the edge of town and, about the time we were ready to move, townsfolk had been complaining about lax security at the school. They were nervous about the place being close to their neighborhoods, and were always suspicious when seeing young men who looked unfamiliar. That certainly meant black kids, because there simply were no blacks around Waukesha then, except the boys in the joint. But I never thought of that, and neither did Bullhead or Chip. We just wanted out.

About 6:30 one summer morning, we skipped out. We probably had about 30 minutes on the staff before they noticed we were missing. Somehow we felt big and important, thought we were big-time hoods. I remember we talked about how they'd probably shoot us if they caught us.

But we had no chance of getting far because people from all over town were calling the institution and the police, telling them that two black boys and an indian had escaped from the home and were running through their neighborhoods. Finally, we ran into a cornfield after being spotted by police.

The officers got on the bullhorn and started shouting. "All right, come out of there. You're surrounded."

"Man, it's all over now," Bullhead said. "They're gonna blow us away."

"Yeah, man," I said. I tried to sound like James Cagney, and I shook hands with my pals and said, "It's been great knowing you."

"They ain't taking me alive," Chip said. "We can get out of here."

Really believing they meant to kill us, we thought we had to flee for our lives. We continued moving through the high corn until we came to the river, and we crossed it. Momentarily, we thought we had given the cops the slip.

What we didn't know all along was that the authorities knew our every move, because somebody from town would call in and report our whereabouts. But I think the law just wanted us to wear ourselves down, and maybe teach us a lesson. As we roamed about the countryside, we became lost. We didn't know where we were, but we'd have to get back into the city limits to get our bearings.

Finally, we made it to a streetcar track and felt if we followed the tracks we could get to Racine or some place where Bullhead had connections. Then from there, I could make it back to Milwaukee.

The three of us got as far as Goerke's Corner the next

day, hungry and half-mad for a drink of water. We were pretty glum by then, thinking that maybe Waukesha wasn't such a bad spot. Bullhead said we'd go to a service station nearby and get some water.

"If we get busted, we get busted," he said.

The owner of the station was cagey. He seemed nice and even bought each of us a bottle of soda pop. But while we were sitting there drinking, he called the police, and in minutes the squad car was there.

The officer didn't even get out of the car. "Hey, you guys," he called. "Come on, get in the car."

There was no reluctance on my part to return to the school, although I did lose my privilege of residing in the honor cottage. Even so, getting arrested again and going back was a relief. On the streets, I was under great tension, drifting from one thing to another, lying to Ma, running from the police. But inside the joint, I didn't have to play those games; I could just be myself.

I still was pretty well behaved inside and earned a furlough, several months from my release. On this furlough, I met a girl I'll call Evelyn. She wasn't a Christian, but was a decent sort of girl and we hit it off. We hit it off too well, however, and she became pregnant. So, immediately upon my release date, we were married. This was in January, 1951, right after I was 18.

My ex-stepfather, who'd worked in a packinghouse for 25 years, got me a job there, and I suppose there were those folks around who thought, "Now with a family responsibility, Buddy's going to settle down."

But they were wrong.

I shot heroin for the first time and nearly overdosed. But the scare at least kept me from mainlining again. So I just went back to burglarizing, drinking and fighting.

During one boosting spree, my friends and I made off with a television set, and for it our fence gave us a 1932 Plymouth—the first car we ever had. However, some girls we were running with thought we made a stupid trade, and they tore the roof off.

But it didn't really matter anyway. Within a couple of

29

days, I ran the car into a tree and totaled it. Considering the fact that I didn't know how to drive, I was lucky I wasn't badly injured.

When my first son was born I was happy and proud, yet not enough to make any real changes in the way I lived. The baby made me feel like a man, yet my lifestyle said that any man could be a father.

Real men—so I thought—loved the street, the crowds, the action. And this man was young enough to enjoy a good street rumble any time.

Chapter **4**

RUNNING WITH LAMES

"Hey, pretty boy.
You ain't gonna be
pretty no more."

One night a neighboring gang grabbed me, and four of them worked me over pretty well in retaliation for a beating one of them had received from the dudes I hung around with. But my crowd felt the severity of my drubbing was too harsh, and they vowed revenge.

One of the leaders of this other group was an Italian kid who prided himself on his good looks. So one night, we got a car and parked it in front of his girl friend's apartment, waiting for him.

It was after midnight when he came bouncing down the stairs, whistling, grinning, a bit high himself. We grabbed him and stuffed him in the back seat of the car and drove off.

After a moment his head cleared. "Hey, man—where are we going?"

We remained silent, except for an occasional, sinister chuckle.

"Come on, you guys—what's happening?" he asked in a shrill frightened voice. "Look, we never meant to come down like that on Buddy. I mean, it was a mistake, huh?"

Seeing his pleading wasn't getting him anywhere, he now tried to turn me toward him. "Look, man, it was a mistake. I'm sorry, you know? It was a bad scene. Here— look, maybe we could go back to my place and have some wine? What do you say?"

No one replied. We enjoyed his terror. And the drive

continued on to a deserted road near the Milwaukee River. We stopped the car, and he struggled mightily to keep us from getting him out of the car.

"Don't drown me, man. That's murder." His face was white with fear.

At this point too, I simply thought we'd kick him around a bit and let it go at that. But one of my boys said, "Man, you'd forget real quick if you was killed. But you ain't never going to forget this."

And while two others held him, he was nailed repeatedly in the face with a broken bottle. Even though the attack sickened me, I laughed with the others, as the victim squirmed and shrieked. We left him on the road, a bloody mess, and went off to get high.

"Hey, pretty boy," a dude shouted back at him, as he lay bleeding and crying on the roadside. "You ain't gonna be pretty no more."

He recovered, and he wasn't pretty no more. And he never again returned to the street wars.

Meanwhile, I managed to provide some sort of living for Evelyn and the three boys we had in our three years of marriage. I kept my job at the packing plant, even though I'd often show up late or drunk—or not at all.

But I also kept boosting and staying high; only now it wasn't so much an adventure. It was a way of life. And a pretty squalid one at that.

Had my Mom not been a Christian, maybe I'd have kept right on the crooked road I was traveling. But in her life, God was always the center.

There were many nights when I'd stop by Mom's place, feeling trapped and wretched, and hear her try to comfort me with words from the Scriptures. Every time I'd see her and complain about my misfortunes, she'd just look at me and say quietly, "Son, why don't you give your life to the Lord? You know that's what He wants. And you'll never find anything in life until you surrender to Him."

As often as not I'd really want to give my life to Christ and know Mom's peace, yet I couldn't and wouldn't. Already I was realizing that life wasn't just a game of cops

33

and robbers. Yet I couldn't cut loose of my friends, so I remained under their influence and pressure, instead of Mom's.

I was in Satan's grip and easily tempted. A friend might say, "Come on, man, here you are, working hard all week for a lousy $90. We can go over here right tonight and pick up $300 or $400. An easy rip-off. You with us or ain't you?"

I never refused, never would let them think me weak or cowardly, when that's really what I was. And all along, so were they.

Through it all there was an awful struggle going on inside me between God and myself. I knew what was going on inside me, but I refused to submit myself to God—or to anyone else, for that matter.

Evelyn sensed impending disaster if I kept on with my usual activities, and she began listening when my mother would come over and try to talk her into joining a church or letting the Lord take over in our lives. Mom believed if Evelyn started church, perhaps I'd follow.

On several occasions we went, and once my wife spoke to me about our involvement with the church. "Maybe if we'd stay with it, we'd get ourselves straightened out," she said.

I may have agreed. I don't remember. But if I did, it was more to get her off my back than anything else.

One afternoon a friend and I were uptown. We wandered into Shuster's Department Store. It had always looked too imposing to boost, so I gave no thought to a rip-off there.

We browsed through the store and then we hit the sidewalk. I was surprised when my friend pulled me aside and said, "Hey, look at these cuff links." Grinning, he dropped them into my hand.

I only had time to catch a single flash of the sun off the highly polished set when a store detective clutched both of us by the wrists. "They are nice, aren't they?" he said coldly. "You boys come with me."

Instinctively, I jerked away and ran. But my friend

called, "Buddy—don't leave me, man."

I returned and belted the detective on the side of his head with a small piece of lead I kept in my pocket for rumbles. With a heavy groan, he caved in, out cold.

"Man, let's move," I shouted, and started off again.

But this was a white neighborhood, and perhaps a dozen people saw me hit that detective. Thinking it was a case of two blacks thumping a white man, about six or eight of them came at us. And they came swinging.

My partner and I were quickly separated. But for a few moments, we managed to hold our own—because we had those pieces of lead.

But we were wearing down quickly, as the fight carried into a dime store next door. The row continued for about five minutes over counters, as displays were scattered and devastated.

Two men hoisted me up and were about to slam me against a counter when I had the sense to give up. Battered and bleeding, I hollered, "Okay, man. I won't fight no more."

They dropped me and, after threatening me, started to walk away. For a moment, I lay on the floor, gasping for breath. But I didn't want to get stuck for damages to the dime store, so I forced myself to get up and walk out of there.

I was almost in the clear, unconcerned about my buddy, when I heard a woman's voice behind me. "That's the one who started it," she cried. "Right there, that colored man."

I glanced back and saw her pointing, as two uniformed officers started toward me. "Stop," one shouted, but I was off and running, eluding them for the moment.

For a while, it looked like I had beaten that rap, and I was home soaking my bruises when a heavy persistent knock came on the door. Even before I opened it, I knew it was the law. And I was right.

"Theodore Jefferson?" said the officer. "You're under arrest."

A firm hand gripped my elbow, and an equally firm voice said, "Come with us."

"Hey, man," I exclaimed. "Be cool, huh? What'd I do?"

The officer simply repeated, "Come on now. Get moving."

Again I was given a break. The judge sentenced me to six months in the workhouse. I figured with time off for good behavior, I'd do only three or four months.

As it turned out, the workhouse was a pretty rough place. Especially if you had to stay inside all the time, as I did. That first day when it was time to go to work everyone else left the dormitory I was in. I ran to the guard and said, "Say, man, where do I go for work?"

The guard looked up my name on his chart and said, "You ain't going nowhere. The people up front think you have too much rabbit blood in you and just might hop away."

So I was confined to the dorm all the while I was there, with little to do but steal the others' cigarettes, mop the floor and lie on my cot.

I hadn't been there six weeks when Evelyn suddenly stopped visiting me. I heard from friends outside that she had started drinking heavily.

And some of her friends convinced her that she was wasting her time with me. I wasn't taking care of her or our boys, and I was running with other women. Further, so they told her, I'd probably spend most of my life in jail.

Evelyn filed for divorce without telling me. I found out some time later when a guard got me and took me downstairs. I went to the office, where a man handed me the notice of a divorce hearing in two weeks. But I would still be in jail by then. I was left powerless to contest the action.

I laughed to mask my shock and fury. "That's okay," I said, tearing up the notice. "Yeah, that's cool."

But inside, I was seething. I didn't expect to get even with Evelyn, but I was thinking, "Man, somebody's going to pay for this. Somebody's going to get hurt.

I did my six months. But the divorce took more out of me than I cared to admit. And after my release, I went to jail many more times that same year on drunkeness and vagrancy charges.

My bizarre behavior was to continue for some time to come—behavior that continually baffled the psychiatrists who examined me in each of the penal institutions I called "home" for varying lengths of time.

One frustrated doctor grabbed me and sat me down in his office. He looked at me and gazed in bewilderment at my chart. Finally he asked, "How is it you're in this place, Jefferson? We're at our wits end trying to figure you out. You shouldn't be here, but you keep coming back, and none of us can figure out why. You're an intelligent young man. You could make something of your life, but you run with lames, man. You're a lame yourself."

What the shrinks couldn't understand was that Satan had a grip on me and was misdirecting my life. They didn't know, or at least didn't say, that the life away from Christ is a life run by Satan.

Actually, I already knew I couldn't ride the fence with God and get away with it. I knew I couldn't hem and haw about how maybe I'd be okay, if I'd pay a little lip service to the Lord. In my heart, I knew it had to be all or nothing.

Because I knew what was the matter with me and was doing nothing about it, my life was in great torment. I rejected what I knew would save me from myself. Instead, I turned into a down and out bum, sleeping on buses or in door stoops and basements of apartment houses—anywhere there was shelter.

Sporadic moments of sobriety were spent panhandling for food or wine, and I lived from one unconsciousness to the next, sustaining the stupor.

I drifted for a full year after my divorce in 1953 before looking for work. Finally, I went to work, landing a job at a plant where tubes were manufactured for boilers.

Now, with a little money coming in, I felt I could return to see my ex-wife and the boys. Evelyn and I discussed getting married again, though it never really was my intention. At this point, I only wanted to get back at Evelyn.

I was already involved with another man's wife. But this lady—I'll call her Gail—was separated from her husband, so I moved in with her. And we started having children of our own—outside marriage.

Meanwhile, I schemed and connived with Evelyn to get her to consider remarrying me. Finally she consented. Though she no longer loved me, she agreed to try again for the sake of the boys.

I set the date and promised I would come by to get the blood test. I knew she'd be telling her friends and family that she and Ted were going to get married again. And I enjoyed a good laugh, thinking about how she'd be hurt when I didn't show up.

Evelyn *was* hurt and, at the time I was pleased. And I soon managed to forget all about her and our sons. I turned my back on my family and left them flat, relinquishing all my rights to my sons. This will cause me deep regret to my dying day. It's a burden I can't dismiss—ever.

As it turned out, Evelyn became an alcoholic, and many years passed before she was able to straighten herself out again. Too, since the time I split from my family, I've seen my sons only once, so I never succeeded in building a relationship with them. Needless to say, they haven't much use for their father—a man who provided nothing for them but grief and abuse.

But when they were still boys, they thought their daddy—the old Ted Jefferson—was cool. I can still see them trying to affect the arrogant swagger I used to carry around myself. That swagger amused me then. But it amuses me no longer, because now it's too late for me to intervene in the lives of my sons, except through the grace of God.

Something else I used to do in those days was to sit on Mom's front steps and think it funny to turn on my younger brothers—kids of 8, 9, and 10. I'd get them drunk or high on grass, and watch them stagger around. The tragedy is that one of those boys—my half-brother is a confirmed alcoholic today. And it's all my fault.

It's a terrible thing for a man to destroy his own life, but it's so much worse when he's helped to destroy others', too. Which is what I did.

In later years, these things would creep into my thoughts as I lay on my bunk in one jail or another. In my mind's eye I could sometimes see those kids stumbling around, acting silly like they would do when I gave them wine. Then I might think of how their lives were ruined.

And there'd be just a twinge of sorrow in my heart, but I always managed to push the feeling back, and stuff those thoughts into a corner of my mind. I would even think, "Why can't I love people? Why can't I love my own family? What kind of person am I? Oh, God, please help me."

But then with the break of a new day it was, "What's happening man? Ain't nothing to it. Give me a joint, man. Let's get high."

Same old big bad Buddy.

I cared for nothing and no one but myself, so I lived for myself, satisfying my desires. I stayed with my present woman, Gail, for five years. And during that time, we had three children. Though we were in love, we never married, in order to keep welfare payments coming in for child support.

But Gail too had been raised in a Christian home and knew we were living in sin, knew that the only way for us to come clean was to surrender to the Lord. There were times we prayed and spoke about getting back in church, going so far as to attend a few services. But I never stayed for long, especially when the preacher said I had to commit myself to God.

No commitment for me, except to myself. What I wanted from God was for Him to leave me alone, so I'd run off and try to get high. Anything to forget about God.

And as long as I was high, I could forget. Not only about God, but about myself and my responsibilities. And so it was, in a doped-up condition one night on the job, I almost lost my life.

I worked nights at the plant, and it was my job, as pipes were hoisted from piles by a lift and conveyed to a vat of acid, to grab the pipes and guide them into the acid. This night, as the pipes came toward me, I grabbed them, and, reeling with blind staggers, almost toppled headfirst into that acid. Somehow I caught myself on the edge of the vat, my nose stopping inches from the smoldering mass.

Here, too, I must have been in the presence of God. It was, I suppose, as if He were saying, as He pulled me back, "Not this time, Ted. I've got work for you yet." God is merciful to us, even when we have turned our backs on Him.

Yet I didn't thank Him for sparing me. I just laughed it off and tried to pretend nothing happened. However, I knew that, had I fallen, I could never have survived that kind of bath.

I never mentioned this incident to Gail, and continued living the way I'd always lived. During these months, I and my friends ripped off record players, clothes and television sets. The materials were easily fenced and brought us money for gambling and drinking.

Then Gail's estranged husband brought things to an end for us, by turning us in for cohabitating. Investigators from the welfare department came in the middle of the night looking for me, and many's the time I bounded from bed in the dead of a winter's night to dive out onto the back porch and shiver for an hour or more in the cold while the house was searched.

Frustrated and angry, I told Gail we'd have to work out another arrangement. I knew some night I'd be too drunk to fly from that bed, and they'd have me. But I wasn't about to move just yet.

One night I'd gone over to Mom's house and found she'd left for a prayer meeting. I stayed around, rapping with the dudes who'd done small burglaries with me before. As usual, we were short on cash.

One dude, the night before, had snatched a purse, but it didn't have nearly enough money for the booze and drugs we wanted, so somebody suggested we hit Mr. Hill's

Cleaners. This was a dry-cleaning establishment occupying the ground floor of Mom's building. We entered the cleaners, but we were already drunk by then and started bumping into things and knocking them over. An area resident, hearing the noise, called the police, who arrived and busted us on the premises.

For this bungled escapade, I got a one-to-three year stretch at the reformatory at Green Bay. And the whole cycle started all over again.

Green Bay had a reputation for being tough, but the only restriction there was the quiet system. Inmates couldn't talk in lines as they waited for meals or instructions.

When I hit the gate at Green Bay my first day, a number of my street buddies were already there. Everyone was saying how great it was to see me again. And that made me feel a bit better, for any prison is scary. There's a lot of talk about how prisons are so-called country clubs. But this simply isn't true. Far from it.

At Green Bay, as at Waukesha, dope and homosexuality were rampant. Guys regularly shot dope on the athletic fields, and homosexuals were getting "married" under the stands. Some men feared going to the shower, so widespread were homosexual advances. For a man was left alone here only if others feared him physically.

As a newcomer to the joint, I was likely prey for some of the older, more experienced inmates. So, knowing I would need it here, I deliberately fostered my reputation for toughness. That meant I was safe, but there were dozens of others who couldn't talk with their fists, and they were subjected to shakedowns and rape almost every day. The whole scene sickened and disgusted me.

I earned my tough reputation in boxing. But I earned it somewhat deceitfully. I'd find some dude who couldn't box well and ask him to go a couple of rounds with me. He'd protest, but I'd tell him I just wanted a little workout and would only tap him.

"Nobody's going to hurt you, man," I'd tell him.

And I'd throw my arm around him and maybe tell him a joke to butter him up. With reluctance, he might agree, and

42

then I'd spread the word around the joint that I would be boxing in a few minutes. There'd be a fair crowd around when we'd start.

"You sure you ain't gonna go all out, man?" the dude would ask.

"No, man. Be cool. Nobody gets hurt."

But once the action started, I'd try to take his head off. I'd have him bleeding and bruised within a few seconds, and all the guys at ringside would say, "Look at Buddy, man. Wow, he's a tough dude. Don't nobody mess with him."

I believed my reputation myself. I talked tough and nobody touched me. I was proud of my ill-gotten notoriety, and other cons respected me for it. But I knew that reputation wasn't me.

I was keeping my emotions inside, and I felt this pressure. Pressure which I now believe was the Word of God, nudging me over to His side. But I fought it and found ways to stay high by sniffing carbon tetrachloride.

I got the carbon tet through my job in the kitchen. I'd drain fire extinguishers into vinegar bottles, and manage to sneak the stuff back to my cell at night, where I'd be off on cloud nine into oblivion.

In the cell next to me was a young immigrant from Hungary. He spoke with a heavy accent and was hard to understand. But one night, after he'd pleaded with me, I promised I'd bring him some stuff that night.

I tried explaining that he should only use a pinch of carbon tet on the corner of a hankerchief, but he soaked the entire handkerchief and put it over his head, then ducked under his blanket.

I heard a gasp, then a cough. Then he screamed, "Oh—I getting stiff. I getting stiff." That was followed by a thick aspirated gurgle and silence.

As he was being carried out, I wasn't thinking about what might have been imminent death for the man. Rather, I was concerned for my own hide. Would they figure out who gave him that stuff and add a load to my sentence if he died?

43

Fortunately, he survived and nobody questioned me. But other pressures were getting to me, and I broke out in festering sores all over my body. That wasn't unusual, for the atmosphere inside a prison is one of constant, crackling tensions.

Any little thing can erupt into an explosion. One day a friend received a divorce notice and cracked up. He tore the toilet from his cell and began throwing everything into the hall. He was subdued finally when a fire hose was turned on him and plastered him unconscious against the wall.

Stuck in a situation like this with time on his hands, an inmate thinks. And because of his depressed state, he probably thinks of revenge on those who've wronged him or of avoiding capture next time around.

Instead of openly breaking down, I was deteriorating mentally. Finally, the doctors recommended isolation for me. And away from the pressures of everyday prison routine, I began to mend.

I did my time, getting released in 18 months. I returned to Gail, but it wasn't the same. People had almost convinced her that I was no good and would soon leave her flat. And the welfare investigators kept prowling around looking for me, wanting me to start with my child support payments.

Finally, I moved out and found myself a rather nice pad in an old ghetto house full of ethnics. It was a congenial sort of multiracial group that had a number of sins in common—drinking, doping, gambling and, on occasion, stealing.

There was a maze of halls in this old house, which at one time had housed the family of a wealthy industrialist, so I'm told. And in each corridor you would be greeted by a mingling of odors from ethnic cooking—chili peppers from the Mexicans, corn bread and black-eyed peas from the blacks, and heavy garlic scents from the Italian's place.

This community consisted of happy-go-lucky crooks and con men, who moved easily into anybody's pad and made themselves at home. Everything went on in that house, including prostitution, and I became a semi-active pimp here, requiring money for dope and gambling, which I was heavily involved in by now.

I continued meeting Gail on the sly, and again she spoke to me about getting married and settling in with a church. While I was in Green Bay, Mom had spoken to her and prayed with her, as she always did with me. I suppose Gail would have gone along with the religion bit if I had.

But I wasn't yet ready for Christianity. That was all right for old folks like Mom. But me? I was too young for that stuff. I wanted to live some more first.

If I could only stay out of jail for a time, why, I'd live my life and there'd be plenty of time for God later. Meanwhile, I was enjoying myself, and I wasn't being hassled for my illegal activities.

My pad was the gambling headquarters and the money would come rolling in, though almost nobody had a legal job. There were nights I'd have a thousand dollars cash, only to blow it on dope for my friends within a couple days. I had money, but it was here today and gone tomorrow.

Though I cared for Gail, I wasn't giving her any money. So again the welfare agents came looking for me, catching me at a low tide. I was broke and got four months in the county slammer for nonsupport.

As soon as I was out, I went back to my place, anticipating getting a job. But I was hooked on alcohol and I loved to smoke marijuana, or take uppers or downers. And I told myself all I'd need was one more good rip-off, maybe one more good high, and I'd be able to get myself together.

But instead of being satisfied, I always had to have one more and one more and one more, and it never ended. I'd come down from a high, and not like what I saw when I looked in the mirror. I knew who I was, and what I'd done, and the only escape was to get high again.

In 1957, I was caught for burglary again. I can't remember the operation at all. I was double stoned. Oh well, I figured, another brief stay in Green Bay. Nothing I can't handle.

Then my parole officer came to see me in the county jail. He just shook his head. I was an old customer. "Ted, you know you're going to be put away, don't you?"

"Yes, I know. Man, I sure hate to go back there." I was tired of the same old things of the reformatory—dope, loneliness, sleepless nights and all the con talk of all the things we used to have.

He blinked and seemed startled. "Ted, you're not going back to Green Bay. You're going to prison. You're going to Waupun."

His announcement hit me like a solid fist in the stomach, and for a moment I couldn't breathe. The big joint! The big time! The realization struck home that this wasn't small-time stuff any more. I was going to the state penitentiary. I would really be a con! A hood!

As I lay on my bunk that night, many thoughts ran through my mind: Where are you going, man? Where are you coming from? What are you going to do now? This thing is getting out of hand. Time, time, time. That's all you've done is time.

Your ex-wife, Gail, your kids—what's life about anyway? God? Jesus? Where is Jesus now? Does God really love sinners? Why do you hate people—and yourself?

Later, brother. Go to sleep. Tomorrow's another day.

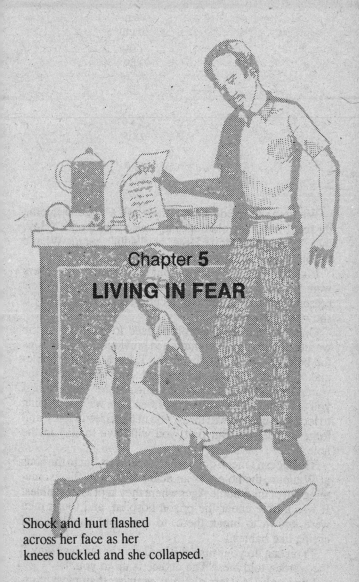

Chapter **5**

LIVING IN FEAR

Shock and hurt flashed
across her face as her
knees buckled and she collapsed.

Waupun surprised me too. There was a sort of welcome for me from all the old dudes in the neighborhood. "Hey, there's young Buddy. How you doin', man? What's happening on the streets?"

Like me, they were losers. But in those days the losers were my kind of people, so I was glad to see them. Their presence gave me a sense of security, and I figured they'd show me the ropes.

One man not the least bit pleased to see me was the warden. I'd earned a reputation in previous incarcerations for being a tough nut to crack. Though not a trouble-maker, I was arrogant and insolent. As I stood facing the warden in his office, he gave me a firm stare. "Jefferson, if you act up here like you did in Green Bay, we're just going to lock you up. We will throw you in the Green House and forget about you. But first, you will have to stay in the hole."

That doesn't mean quite what it seems to, but to the cons at Waupun, the hole was an actual dungeon—like something out of the Middle Ages where they kept incorrigibles. It was a hole under the prison hospital, and tough men were known to break there, to come out babbling and crying like babies.

"You can do your time the hard way or the easy way," the warden told me. "The choice is up to you."

I was only 24 years old then, younger than most hardcore cons. Again, my youth made me a prime target for homosexual advances. It got so bad, I hated to go to work. I was assigned duties in the kitchen and had to carry pails of food from table to table and scoop food onto each man's plate. As I'd make my rounds I was confronted with all manner of disgusting and obscene propositions. If the good Lord hadn't endowed me with boxing ability, I'm sure I'd have been subjected to numerous indecent attacks.

Since I was a new prisoner, I was put in a dormitory instead of a cell. Maybe the officials thought they were doing me a favor, but they weren't. That dorm was one of the meanest places I'd ever been. We slept in a crowded open bay with all the beds pushed close together. And there was only a small toilet area with no partitions, so privacy was absolutely impossible. Without mentioning details, I can't imagine a sicker society than I was part of during those early days at Waupun.

In desperation, I went to the prison psychiatrist and told him to send me across the tracks where the state mental hospital was located. I told him I just couldn't handle what I came up against every day in the prison. But instead, he let me be assigned to a cell block that housed older, rougher cons. At least in a cell, I got a semblance of privacy.

Also in that same cell block were two men from home. My old buddy Rudolph who had hit the cleaner's place with me was still doing time. And so was an ex-stepfather who had gotten busted for some sort of con game.

They managed to show me the ropes on the inside and were always available to talk to. But still, I never did get used to that place. For, inside any penal society, there were vicious men who would kill a man for just a couple packs of cigarettes.

The brutal attacks on weaker inmates were common-place, and to this day I can still hear those screams of terror and frustration. Yet, because of the unwritten code among cons, nothing was done to stop the attacks. No con who values his life ever becomes a snitch. He snitches and he may well get his throat cut. So he quietly absorbs the assaults—and lives.

By keeping my nose clean I was sent to the honor farm at Lac du Flambeau. Things were somewhat normal there and the air was clean. The work in the woods was good, and I took pride in my tasks. I had time for reflection there too, and though I occasionally thought of the Lord—usually after a visit from my long-suffering mother—I still preferred avoiding Him.

At this time too, I was attempting more intellectual pursuits. I started reading mythology and other forms of religion such as Hinduism, Shintoism and, along with many other blacks, experimented with Muslim philosophy. I'd do anything, it seemed, to stay away from the Lord. Satan was a powerful persuader, and since none of the other religions required me to submit, I found them much more agreeable than Christianity.

I believed that the white Jesus and His followers formed an oppressive religion to keep blacks in slavery. I knew God was real, but still reasoned that His religion was there to keep the black man in chains. The real point of Christianity wasn't clear to me, for in my confused state I viewed the black Christian as the ultimate Uncle Tom, bowing and saying, "Yes, massah," every time whitey kicked him.

I'd heard all about black preachers telling us how things would be better in heaven, but I wanted things now. The white people—a great many of them anyway—were and still are using their Christianity wrongly. And I'd seen enough of those Christians. The Negro spiritual goes, "When I get to heaven, gonna put on my shoes," but I noticed whitey already had his shoes and he wasn't in heaven yet.

By this twisted logic, I could forestall the power of Jesus from opening my heart. And I did this, even though I observed the transforming power of God in the few cons in prison who'd been converted. I knew too, that there was no such thing as true rehabilitation in prison; that required

nothing less than submission to the Lord. And I wasn't ready to submit.

Of that three-year sentence, I served 19 months. And how, during that time, I wanted to taste freedom again. I had been miserly while in the joint, scrimping and saving $300 from my meager wages and from craft items I'd sold.

That $300 was no big bundle, to be sure, but it could sure buy one big drunk—which was all I wanted. One big blast to celebrate my release, then maybe look for a job. Anything was possible.

I got out and made my way to a place called Hooligan's Bar in Milwaukee and danced in. "Hey, man," I said, flashing my roll, "Buddy's buying for the house." I shot a remark at the women lined up at the bar and then stepped up to the bar myself.

A number of people toasted me, slapped me on the back. "Buddy's buying, baby, not begging."

Everyone laughed, but at least one of them waited. I poured down the gin as fast as the man could set it up, and it wasn't long before the limbs went numb and I passed out. While unconscious I got rolled—a trick I'd pulled countless times myself—and lost all my money. I vowed I'd kill the man who took that money if I ever found him. I could make that idle threat because I was quite certain I'd never find out. In all probability though, it was one of my "friends" from the bar.

I hadn't been out of Waupun a week when I met Kenny, a nightclub singer, who was my sister's present boyfriend. He was a talented musician, definitely on the way up, and he impressed me because he'd let me come into the club and sign his name on the tab.

One evening, after we closed down the club, we headed back to my sister Alice's apartment and found three men from Chicago in the house hassling her. An argument followed, and Kenny and I threw all three of them down the stairs.

A couple hours later, after we'd eaten and gotten high smoking pot, we assumed the outsiders had left. So we started down to the parking lot. But the three dudes had laid an ambush for us, and as Kenny turned to go into the lot, he was nailed with a two-by-four across the nose. He went down. As I turned, I was hit on top of the head; it felt like my skull had split.

One of the men was screaming, "Kill that sucker, man," and I was about to get cracked again, when Kenny got up. Instead, the attacker turned back on him and smashed him in the same spot, breaking his face open. Then that dude turned again toward me and was about to crack me once more, when a car pulled into the lot, scaring the men off.

Not until two hours later were we discovered by my brother who had come to the house. Kenny was taken to the hospital and patched up, but his singing career was over. I refused attention because I thought I'd get my parole revoked if the fight was reported. But later in the week, while drunk, I was taken to the emergency room and treated for infection, while the intern put eight stitches in my head.

Now I was not only broke, but seriously wounded as well.

Gail's uncle—I'll call him Dan—was also my brother-in-law, being married to Corrine. I had always admired his cool. He was a high-stakes gambler, carried a pistol and kept plenty of women at one time. But now he was just a street hustler too, so he helped me score on a couple of burglaries.

By this time, I was living in constant fear, for burglary was now my way of life. And in order to overcome that fear, it was necessary for me to stay high. So Dan kept me drinking. The two of us spent considerable time snorting heroin and downing Thorazine and Benzedrine.

The two of us branched into the old Murphy game, designed to rip off white men. They were easily duped. We'd lead a white dude into a black neighborhood, promising him black women. Then we'd ask him to produce identification to prove he wasn't from the police vice squad.

As soon as the man reached for his wallet, one of us would hit him while the other snatched his wallet, and we'd be off and running through the many mazes of hallways and rooftops only those familiar with the turf would know. We'd then celebrate our good fortune by all-night drinking and snorting bouts.

If any money was still left after that, we'd gamble. And the gambling was usually done at my place, where the booze flowed like water, and music blared into the wee hours. It was a regular fleshpot, and my activities there were hardly Christian. But that was the whole idea—I could get high, roll dice, play cards, listen to music and not have to think about how I was defying God. At least, not until I'd come down off the high and had to pull another job. It was a vicious circle.

I was now 28 years old and—in the minds of my mother's friends and Gail's family—going nowhere except back to jail and straight to hell. But while all that was true, I determined to do neither right away.

For the present, however, going back to jail remained the greater threat. And I had a number of close calls. For every so often, while attempting burglaries, I'd find myself arrested. And every time I was, I'd get on my knees and pray, asking God to keep me out of jail. I'd promise Him that I'd straighten out if I could avoid another term in prison.

There were several times when I managed to get off without a rap, but even on those occasions, instead of keeping my promise to the Lord and trying to come to grips with my wasted life, I'd return to the old arrogant posture so well known to my friends.

"Man, you should have seen me in there," I'd boast after coming out of court. "Just like Clarence Darrow, man. Had the judge eating out of my hand."

Exit the Lord from my life again. But enter Marie.

At one of my gambling parties, a young girl of 17 wandered in with a friend. I was rolling the hot dice that night, so like a big shot, I peeled off a hundred dollars and told her to go downtown and buy herself some new clothes.

Immediately, I felt like a heel. I wanted that girl, but at the same time, I told myself I'd already ruined a number of other lives. So why would I want to do the same to this young girl?

Yet that is exactly what I did, and it wasn't long before she discovered she was pregnant. Clearly though, I felt no responsibility toward her, nor, for that matter, toward anyone. So, characteristically, when she told me, I split.

I still had ties with Gail, and I didn't want further ties with this new girl. I thought maybe her family or someone would get her an abortion. In any case, I didn't want to have to think about it.

But I had reckoned without Mom. Finally, I'd gone too far, even for my long-suffering mother who'd always provided me a haven of rest and who'd always taken me in and fed me, who'd always listened to me and tried to counsel me in the ways of the Lord. This girl, Marie—who is now my wife and whose fine Christian witness helped sustain me and my family through the many crises that were to come—found Ma's home and, in tears, told her what had happened.

"You've got a lot of bad in you, Buddy," Ma told me when I stopped by later. "But I never thought you'd ruin a nice young girl like that." And she threw me out of her house.

That was only the beginning of my present problems. I was already missing support payments to two other women, and now this new situation had developed.

An angry social worker gave me a thorough dressing down one afternoon. "Who do you think you are?" he demanded. "Going around and getting all these women messed up? Who's supposed to pay for all this carrying on? You keep this up and you'll spend the rest of your life doing three-month stretches in the workhouse."

I might have laughed it all off, but this girl was a minor, and this time I figured the court would just throw me away. For, in addition to everything else, contributing to the delinquency of a minor would give them an excuse to shut me up for a long time. So, after a few days wrestling with my conscience, well-oiled with liquor, I made a decision.

I got a tiny apartment for Marie, and told her that I'd

marry her. But in the meantime, I added, I'd be gone for a while, tending to business out of town. My business was gambling, and there were times when I'd be away for two or three weeks at a time.

Then I went to Gail's house and set her up with the same story. I promised her a new living room suite if I won big. What crossed my mind then was to simply light out, get away from Milwaukee and lose myself and my past somewhere else.

But I liked Milwaukee and I dug the action there. So, finally, before the birth of our child, I married Marie. Things went well for a while, but I was always plagued with the nagging realization that sooner or later I'd have to tell Gail I was already a married man.

I hadn't seen her in over a month, but when I came in, she just said, "I'm glad to see you're finally home." And she started to fix me something to eat.

All I wanted to do was just tell Gail I was married to someone else and leave. For I didn't want to mistreat my young wife. Marie had not yet grown bitter, and she retained a quality of innocence. I now felt a responsibility for her.

Gut Gail had borne three of my children. What about her? Man, what a terrible mess. And it was all of my making.

Finally in great agitation, I blurted, "Gail, I'm married now."

She didn't even turn to look at me, and she laughed as she worked. "Aw, you know you're kidding. You sure do like to kid. You know you're not going to marry anybody but me."

Though the pressure was searing my guts, I forced a laugh and agreed with her. But a few minutes later I said again, "I'm really married." I stood up and whipped out my marriage license.

I'll never forget the shock and hurt that flashed across her face. Her knees buckled and she collapsed. It was like dropping a clock on the floor and watching it fly apart.

Gail lay on the floor a few seconds trying to catch her

breath. Then sobbing violently, she cried out, "Why, Buddy, why? You know I love you. How can you do me like this?"

I gritted my teeth and said, "I can't stand this. I'm leaving." And I left her there broken, totally disspirited. I was the cause of her anguish, but I sure wasn't going to sit there and watch her disintegrate. Yet as I left her, I thought, "Man, you are nothing but a rat."

Later, Gail fell in with lesbians and prostitutes and began running with married men.

If I cared about all this, it was only a twinge of conscience. I had other problems of my own that needed tending. For I was now responsible for the financial support of three families—Evelyn's, Gail's and Marie's.

These families would always argue with me. And as I look back, their arguments were pathetically heart-breaking. One of my boys once told me, "You love them more than us. You're ashamed of us." And as he started crying, I turned my back, and, as I'd done so often before, simply walked away.

The thought of my family burdens kept me on booze and drugs. I stayed high to avoid the awful reality I'd arranged for myself. It was pointless for me to work because I couldn't earn enough to support one family, let alone the nine children I'd fathered by now.

In the midst of my constant emotional turmoils, during my infrequent moments of sobriety, I sensed an inner voice tugging gently, with the request to "Come unto Me. Come unto Me." I almost gave in, but was always able to resist.

Though not willing to admit my mistakes and start a new life, I did find a job, which at least kept food on the table. And I was back in Mom's good graces. It was at this time that she started urging Marie and me to go to church.

She owned a small building now and rented the ground floor to a Pentecostal congregation, and we started attending services there. I found myself enjoying the companionship and fellowship of true believers. I felt a warmth and security and a feeling of optimism that things would finally turn out right.

Because of my influence in the neighborhood, I got a circle of young people involved in that church, attending Bible study and prayer meetings, in addition to regular Sunday services. There were over a dozen young adults who were active, and at last it seemed the Lord was going to direct my energies for His use. But I still wouldn't give Him full surrender.

One evening, Rev. Lovell Tyler was having a baptismal service in the church. And the power of the Holy Spirit was among us. We had no lovely baptistry in the front with a beautiful serene painting. Ours was something like a watering trough and was located in the basement. But it was beautiful all the same, and the atmosphere was so alive that you felt as if you might reach out and literally get a grip on the Holy Spirit.

It was time for me to make a decision for the Lord. While a big part of my previous existence had been centered on drugs and sex, those temptations now seemed behind me. I thought I was ready at last to become a new creature.

So that night, that entire young adult group received baptism. When Marie emerged from the water, she became the most beautiful woman I'd seen before or since. Peace and joy filled the room.

But when I was immersed, I didn't feel the Holy Spirit. And the reason was that I wouldn't let Him in. The only thing I felt was envy for my brother who came out of baptism shouting God's praises aloud. Joy radiated from him. I wanted what he had.

"How come he got it so fast?" I wondered. But, at the same time, the devil was nudging me and saying, "Man, to make this commitment, you're going to have to give up your women, your pot and those other things." I was weak, and the lure of the world remained strong, so I listened to the devil and gave only a part of myself to God.

But while I felt no immediate temptations for the old

58

lusts, Satan had thrown up a new stumbling block—envy. And I was falling for it.

I knew though, what transformation Christ could make in a man or woman. I once knew a prostitute who had received Christ as her own Savior. And that woman, receiving courage and strength from the Holy Spirit, was able to resist threats from her pimp and refused to return to sin. I recognized she was strong enough in the Spirit to resist anything.

"You can beat me or kill me, but praise the Lord, I'm through," she told her pimp, as he stood with a knife threatening her. He left her alone.

In the weeks to come, I thought that I'd be all right too. After all, I told myself, an occasional joint shared with a few friends, a little gambling never hurt anything. Besides, I never missed church and Bible study.

Rev. Tyler saw me beginning to backslide. He called me aside one evening after prayer meeting. "You know, Buddy, I ain't saying this just to scare you, but if you backslide, you're going to take all these other young folks with you. And you know it. It ain't going to be pleasing to the Lord."

He showed me 2 Peter 2:22 where it says if a fellow has been cleansed and he returns to sin, it's like a dog eating its own vomit. "Give a hog a bath," said Rev. Tyler, "and it goes right back to the mud and slime. Now if this happens to you, you'll never have a peaceful day as long as you live."

I knew he was right, but I didn't know how soon his prophecy would come true. Anyway, I thought I wasn't responsible for those people. I had my own troubles to worry about.

Like Cain, I thought, "Am I my brother's keeper?"

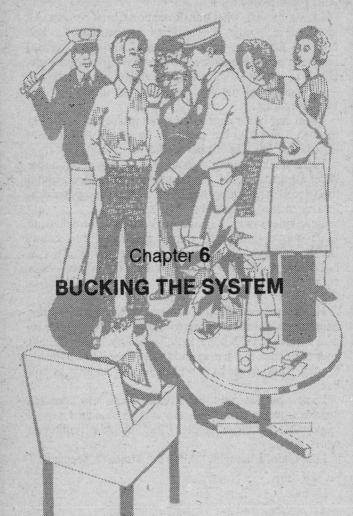

Chapter 6

BUCKING THE SYSTEM

The cop pointed to the puddle.
"You don't have a kidney
problem, do you?"

One Sunday, after morning church services, I was home spending a quiet day with my family. It was about a week after Rev. Tyler had confronted me, and we were sitting around the table after dinner just talking about how nice it was to be together and back with the Lord. But this pleasantness was not to last.

Garmon Harrison, an old non-Christian friend formerly married to my sister, Alice, came over. Garmon had just purchased a new car, so he stopped by to ask if I wanted to go for a ride with him. There seemed little harm that could come from a car ride, so I agreed.

We stopped by Lake Michigan on this lovely summer afternoon and watched some fishermen surf cast. Nearby, mothers scolded youngsters for running too close to the water.

After we had stretched our legs for a while, we got back in the car to head home. Garmon pulled a bottle of wine from under the seat and took a long swallow, then looked at me. He knew I had gotten active in the church again, but he said, "You didn't want one, did you? Ain't nothing wrong with a little sip."

The devil won out again as I took the bottle and, in short order, helped Garmon polish it off. We then followed the wine with a six-pack of beer, and I knew that church no longer mattered in my life. I'd do whatever I pleased.

After that, the rest was easy. I stopped attending church,

and started in on drugs again—turpenhydrate (a codeine cough syrup), pot, heroin—whatever I could find that would keep me from thinking about how I'd failed God again.

Then Rev. Tyler's predictions started coming true. My brother's wife lost her baby, and my brother suspected her of seeing another man. Eventually my brother and his wife drifted from the church and were divorced. Meanwhile, another fellow from our group contracted TB and was hospitalized.

I abandoned my family and tried to re-establish myself with Gail. And my wife, due no doubt to my neglect, started getting arrested herself on minor charges, such as being in a tavern under the legal age. Complicating things, Gail had another of my children, and I was tossed in the slammer for continued nonsupport.

At least in jail I was away from the pressures of the life I lived on the outside. And there was a measure of peace—or so I thought—until the day both Gail and Marie turned up to visit me at the same time and started a row. I knew I had gotten into a quagmire from which there was no human escape.

Some years later, Gail was to meet with a violent death. (A jealous wife, upon spotting Gail with her husband in a gambling joint, shot her in the head.) Gail died instantly, leaving our three children to fend for themselves, bouncing from one foster home to another.

Looking back, I believe it was the grace of God that saw me through. Even then, He was going to fulfill the promise my mother made to Him those long years ago in that rickety log cabin.

I wasn't thinking of that then, of course, and sought the only escape available to me—drugs, which I could get in the county jail and in any other jail or prison I've ever been in.

After a few months, I was released and back running with my loose crowd. The pattern seldom varied, a burglary or con game would sometimes secure large sums of money to be squandered on drink, drugs, gambling and women. Then when the cash flow ebbed, we'd start the cycle all over again.

One cold, snowy night in February, 1961, two friends and I were staggering home, drunk as usual. Customarily, one of the men helped pay his rent by loading a coal hopper each midnight. But this night he was so blind drunk, he wouldn't have been able to lift the coal shovel if he could have found it. So we decided to help him do his job.

Just off the basement in this building where he worked was a stockroom for a clothing store. And somehow the stockroom door had been left open, so when one of our number fell against it, it opened.

"Say, man, dig all these clothes. We can really make a bundle," said one of my partners, as we ran into the big room filled with high quality merchandise.

Our criminal minds feasted upon the racks and racks of coats, hats, suits and a few fur coats. Normally we'd have gotten a truck and taken the entire stock, as we had done before. But it was late tonight, and we were stoned out of our minds anyway.

Even so, I was already thinking of what I'd tell Marie when I got home. I'd been gone four days this time, and she'd be mad, so I picked out two of the most expensive coats I could find.

"I've been gambling, baby," I planned to tell her, "and won big. But these dudes didn't have enough money to pay up, so they made their wives give me these coats."

The excitement of the prospective heist started sobering us. "Man, this is too good to be true," I said. "Let's get down to business. But be cool, you dudes, and don't overload yourselves. We don't want to get busted."

We hadn't sobered enough. So instead of following my advice and taking one or two items each, we all got greedy and loaded up, staggering under the weight of the expensive furs and garments. With our loot, we crept outside in the dead of night.

A friend of ours lived just three blocks away, and we only had to cross two intersections before we could hit an alley and bound up the fire escape to his pad. I placed my

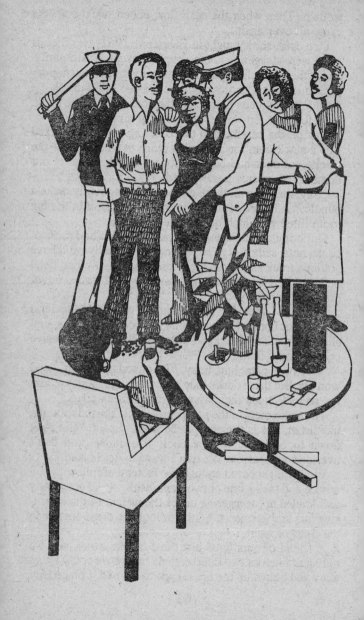

bundle on the sidewalk and sneaked to the first inter-section, looking up one street and down the other.

I signalled the other two to follow. "Come on, you guys. The coast is clear."

I repeated the procedure at the next intersection. "If we get past this one," I told myself, "we're home free. Once across here, we can dart into the alley and follow that to the fire escape."

Though I didn't know it, an officer was in the street. But at the moment I looked out, he had stepped into a door stoop to check a lock.

"Okay, man," I whispered. "Everything's mellow—you dig? Let's make it!"

We all dashed across and into the alley, laughing wildly because we'd made it so easily. Still drunk and uncommonly noisy, the three of us were hooting and slapping each other on the back. Then we started ambling down the alley, singing, secure with the stolen goods.

Suddenly, that officer was directly behind me. "All right, you guys, stop or I'll shoot."

And I'm thinking, "Oh no, I can't go back to that jail again. Later for this turkey! But now I've got to move fast."

And I moved fast. Turning quickly, I dumped my load on the officer and split. It took him a second or two to free himself of the merchandise, and then those footsteps were behind me again. "Stop! This is your last warning. I'll shoot."

The others had made it—now it was between the cop and me. The shot rang out and pinged off the bricks of two buildings. But in that instant, I'd managed to turn the corner and bound up that fire escape into the apartment where a party was in progress.

"I lost my loot, but at least I'm safe," I assured myself. I won't be in jail tonight, that's for sure."

"Man, we're safe," I said, noticing my two buddies had also made it. But we hadn't been in the room more than 15 minutes when someone was beating on the door. "Open up—police."

There were maybe 10 people in the place, and two

officers started questioning everybody. "How long have you been here?" a young patrolman asked me.

"Since early morning," I said. "Three, maybe four hours."

He nodded. then I noticed him looking down at my feet. I cast a furtive glance downward and saw puddles around my shoes from the freshly melted snow. I tried acting nonchalant, but thought to myself, "How stupid can I get?"

"Wait a minute," the cop said. "If you've been here three or four hours, how come there's water on the floor by your feet? You don't have a kidney problem do you?"

Everyone stood around trying to look cool. They didn't want to excite The Man, as he would then want to look the place over. And we all knew that if he did, he'd find the drugs I had stolen from a place on the west side.

So I had to play my role as Mr. Super Cool. I had to act as I thought others saw me. No matter what was in my heart and mind—fear, hate for these cops, the impulse to flee blindly past them to freedom—I had to act tough.

But with all the stuff hidden in the same room, I wanted to get out of there—fast. And I knew there was no evidence yet for an arrest, so I said, "Stop messing with me, man. If you're going to take me downtown, let's go."

He glared at me, then addressed all of us. "I'm taking everybody downtown."

"This is cool, too," I thought. "I'll be home in an hour."

Except that one of my buddies in tonight's looting escapade was with me in another burglary some months before and had left a thumbprint on a gas station cash box. Given a promise of leniency for the earlier gas station job, he fingered me for the clothing store heist. The other man corroborated his story.

At the time of their turning me in, I knew nothing of it. So I was left the only one holding out, the only one who wouldn't admit involvement. And I was the only one to be sent up.

There is no honor among thieves. Especially when they get busted.

It looked like I was on the old merry-go-round again. And topping things off, Marie was expecting another child. "But for once," I thought, "I might be able to use my family in getting me off the hook."

When I entered the courtroom, my two partners whispered, "Probation," and nodded reassuringly to me. The judge read the charge and my lawyer, the public defender, said a few words—all very official and routine. The judge then asked me if I'd like to say anything before he passed judgment.

Time to try the old con game again. "Well, Your Honor," I began, hanging my head a bit to look contrite, "I'd like to appeal for probation. You see, I have a wife and family, and I love them. My wife's expecting another baby.

That old, mild-mannered judge shot out of his chair. "Since when did you love your wife?" he shouted, pointing his finger at me. "Since when do you love anybody? You've been on welfare nearly a year—you don't want to work. Your record is—well, I've never seen anything like this.

I sentence you to not less than one year and not more than five years at hard labor at Waupun, Wisconsin." He sat down, his face flushed. "Get this man out of my courtroom."

It dawned on me then that the other two had snitched on me, and I was filled with hatred. I knew the day would come when I'd kill both of them.

In fact, back at the joint, I told a few felons I trusted that when those bums came through I'd kill them both in prison. I knew they'd be coming through Waupun sooner or later because everything they did in life pointed to an eventual trip to the penitentiary.

Finally, one did get busted and was sentenced to Waupun, and I was pleased. But, fearing for his life, he begged the warden to send him back to Green Bay. In an unprecedented move, the warden agreed with him.

I was older now; I knew my way in the world of the con and had learned the ropes of the system. I really thought that this time, finally, my running days had ended. I thought about my past and felt some remorse for what I'd done, though I think my sorrow was not so much for what I'd done, but because I'd been caught again.

As usual, Mom would come on visiting days to pray with me and read the Bible. Her eyes filling with tears, she again assured me that God loved me and cared for me and, no matter what I'd done, He could wipe it all away if I'd only turn to Him. And Marie too, though I didn't deserve her loyalty, stood by me and visited regularly, bringing news of the children and home.

While I hadn't softened entirely, I began to think about my family. And I thought how awful it was for a man to be nearly 30 years old and not know his family. No, I wasn't about to turn to God, but I did think about my future. And my reading habits changed from pornography to biographies and quality books.

But I was still into drugs, meeting a guy in prison who was convicted as a dealer on the outside and who simply continued his trade on the inside. He supplied me with pills. And I took a good supply with me when I was sent to Lake Geneva, a pre-release center, where I was assigned to the maintenance crew. I worked in the boiler room and enjoyed relative freedom.

When my parole came after 30 months, I was given a welder's job with a boiler company in Milwaukee. I worked steadily now, but I still messed with drugs. And though it was a wretched thing to do, I even conned my wife into smoking pot with me.

Marie had waited all that time for me while I was in prison. And now, simply to keep from losing me again, she agreed to get into the drug scene with me. Not content with ruining myself, I was out to make life as miserable as possible for those close to me.

But I was productive and built up a good work record at the boiler company. I was earning roughly $170 a week, which wasn't bad money back in 1964. Yet even that incentive didn't keep me from pulling jobs within a month of my release.

"Hey, man, we're going to rip off this place," a buddy told me. "You want to come along?"

I quickly agreed, though a tug of conscience seemed to say, "Hey, you're just aching to go back to Waupun, ain't you?"

There were other pressures too. I had support payments totalling over $200 a month, and I also had to support my present family, now numbering four children. I felt I had to rob to live, and rob I did.

In my criminal career, I figure hundreds of thousands of dollars worth of goods and money passed through my fingers. But there was never anything to show for it. I was always on the edge of or in the midst of poverty. Easy come—easy go.

There came a point in 1966 when I almost straightened around, but a welfare agent's attitude squelched it. I had defaulted on a support payment. I hadn't robbed in some time and hadn't been able to work overtime. I tried to explain to the agent the circumstances I was in. I told him frankly, that in order to support my family now, I'd have to steal to make ends meet.

"We don't care about this wife and family," he said coldly. "I don't care how many kids you have at home. You take care of these others first. I could care less for the ones you got now. They are your problem, not mine."

I was stunned, and Marie was badly scared. "So, we're nothing, huh?" she said. "The Man says we're nothing— worse than nothing. We don't count." Angry tears welled up in her eyes. "I guess we never were anything—and never will be."

"Wait a minute, baby," I said. "I never said that. Not me."

But that confrontation put a block between us, and the marriage began to sour. This incident also gave me an added excuse to hate the white man's so-called society.

I had worked hard, trying to be on the level, yet it seemed that the system always worked against me. And I felt that God was against me, bringing me trouble when I was really trying. Finally I thought, "What's the use—I've had it."

There seemed no point in working any more. So, after three years at the boiler plant, I quit. Which didn't help matters at home. Marie and I argued long and loud, and the kids were crying and frightened half the time.

The only thing for me to do was stay high, to keep numb in a stupor. For whenever I'd come down, I'd be hostile and angry.

Finally one night, after hours of drinking in a dive appropriately named The Hole, I staggered out into the middle of the street and cursed God for 10 minutes. I defied Him, challenged Him to strike me down dead.

Onlookers laughed and cheered, as I emptied my vengeful spleen at Almighty God. Yet, in His infinite mercy, He spared me. He knew that Ted Jefferson's time had not yet come, that Ted Jefferson had work to do. And though I did not want to accept it at the time, I knew it would be the Lord's work.

I guess all through my life to this point, there was always that gentle tugging at my heart by the Holy Spirit. Deep down within—even then—I knew that I was to preach the gospel one day, to do the work of an evangelist.

But I was like Jonah who fled from the presence of the Lord. And like Jonah, I too would go into the depths of that "mighty tempest in the sea." But Jonah was sucked under and swallowed by a great fish sent by God to punish him. I was soon to be dragged under and drowned by the weight of my own sin.

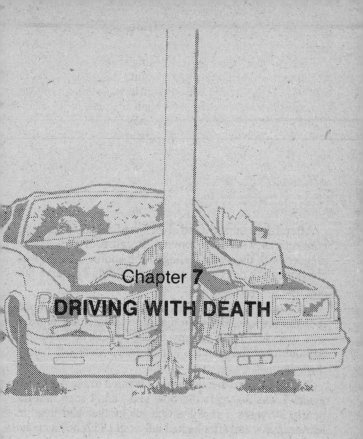

Chapter **7**

DRIVING WITH DEATH

I came to, my face smashed
against the dash.

After I had cursed God, I believed I had severed all connections with Him forever. Because of this, I was plagued with the awful feeling of impending death. I was convinced my days were numbered. I didn't deserve life and had actually given up hope.

I thought that before long I'd be snuffed out in some foolish escapade. But even that didn't matter any more. I was tired and reckoned my family would be better off without me. I'd done little to make their existence happy anyway.

Before I was to die, however, I wanted to see my father again. I was 34 years old now and hadn't seen him for nearly 30 years. I recalled that his mother had lived in Minneapolis, and after he had left us in 1937, he had gone back there to be with her.

I knew some people in the Twin Cities. When you've bounced around prisons long enough, you're bound to make acquaintances from everywhere. So I boarded a bus for St. Paul, calling on friends there who allowed me to crash for a few days, and who supplied me with booze and pot and parties for about a week.

I mentioned to one of my friends that I had a father who lived in Minneapolis, and I believed he was living in a new highrise. This man said there was a fairly new highrise on Olson Highway, and he drove me over there one afternoon. I went in and found the name Theodore Jefferson on a mailbox.

Not knowing what I would say or what to expect, and feeling anxious and uncomfortable, I went upstairs and rang his bell. A woman answered the door and let me in. Inside, I recognized my Dad carrying on, high in the midst of a party.

He didn't recognize me, but didn't ask who I was either. He thought I was just another cat wanting to get high or to find a woman to use for a while.

He looked at me through dull, glazed eyes. "How you doin'?" he slurred. "Have a drink."

Somebody brought me one and I sat opposite my father, listening to him curse and tell risque stories that made everyone laugh. Like mine, his life in the past 30 years had been wasted pimping and drinking.

And as I looked at Dad, I thought, "this can't really be my father. Not this drunk." I hadn't stopped to think that I was a chip off the old block—a drunk myself.

After a time the party began to wind down, and several people left. I approached Dad then. "Ain't you got a boy somewhere?" I asked.

He frowned and put down his glass. "Yeah, I got a boy in Milwaukee somewhere," he growled softly. "But he likes his Mama. He stays with her."

"How do you know?" I asked. "Have you ever seen him to talk to?"

"Well," he said. "they tell me he's some kind of gangster or somethin'. I guess he's probably doin' time right now."

He took a long swallow from his drink, burped loudly and forced a smile. "His Mama, she never let me near the kids. Turned them all against me."

Now he was tearing into Ma, telling how she'd mistreated him during their marriage, how hard life had been for him and how it was impossible to live up to the expectations she and her family had set for him.

"A man's got to let loose once in a while," he said.

"Ain't natural hanging around with Holy Rollers all the time."

He continued blaming Ma for the misfortunes that befell him over the years, cursing and swearing, until finally I managed to get in a question. "This boy, is his name Ted, like yours?"

He stared at me and said nothing, a puzzled frown on his face. "How do you know about him?"

I shrugged and returned his stare.

There was a moment of tense silence, then Dad recognized me and clapped his hands. "Well, hi, Teddy Boy," was all he said, and he chuckled. He turned to someone else and said, "Somebody get him a girl. Let him have a taste of Minneapolis."

I was shocked, though I didn't show it. I thought he might welcome me with open arms and we would develop the relationship we never had. Instead I felt like I'd been kicked in the stomach. But I kept my cool and helped myself to another slug of Scotch.

The girls who came in were recent escapees from a state hospital, and right away I started in pimping. Along with pimping, came the attendant crimes of mugging the johns and sometimes beating them unmercifully.

I also started stealing again, and to keep things clean, I got myself an ID in the name of Arnold Jefferson, because I knew it wouldn't be long before the Wisconsin authorities would be after Ted Jefferson for nonsupport and parole violations.

To keep up the good front I landed a low-paying job with a barrel factory on Plymouth Avenue and earned about $1.50 an hour there, working with winos. But all the real action was at night with the girls and the usual street crimes. I stayed high day after day, and it didn't matter at the factory because so did all the other employees.

Time slipped by quickly, and I had been in the city about two months. For some reason I stayed on in Minneapolis, though my original plan had been to see my father, then move to California.

I had found a small room in a boardinghouse run by an

old black brother named George Warren. The house was little more than a crash pad for numerous drunks and drifters. But George Warren was not your ordinary flophouse manager. He was a dedicated Christian, and his kindliness was not lost on all the derelicts who phased in and out of there over the years.

George tried to witness often, but where I was concerned, he didn't have to; I already knew. My problem was in trying to forget God, my family and my past. Except there was no forgetting, unless I was high—a condition I strove mightily to perpetuate.

I remember little of the next weeks, except that some people I knew were set to go to Detroit, and I had agreed to go along. Detroit was a great city for hustling, they said. Plenty of easy money and drugs. I quit my job on a Friday, and was set to leave on Sunday.

That same Friday night in April, 1966, I met a fellow in a neighborhood tavern. He was also a street hustler, who recognized in me a kindred spirit. He'd probably seen me operate in the various joints in the black community.

Perhaps he was a bit timid about engaging in a rip-off of this sort on his own, so he approached me with "Hey, man, there's this white dude in the club next door who's got a lot of bread. You game for getting a little of it?"

I jumped at the chance. "Might as well rip the honky off, man," I said.

We left together and found the man half-drunk in the small bar. First order was a black woman whom we procured, and the group of us bounced from place to place throughout the night, finally ending up in an illegal after-hours dive. By this time we had fleeced the man of a large sum of money, all the while convincing him that we were his friends.

As the night wore on into morning, folks were getting sick and passing out until only a few of us were still around to keep things lively. Even we were in pretty sad shape. And if I'd had any sense, I'd have left hours before. But Satan works on a man's mind, makes him greedy. Under his influence I never had enough money, enough booze, enough dope, enough women. There wasn't enough self-gratification.

I noticed the man put the remainder of his bankroll in his coat pocket, so I asked him for a ride home. I figured once we were in his car, I'd be able to take the rest of his money too.

We got in the car. My head buzzed, but I kept my mind on that wad of green in his pocket. This dude was higher than I, and I should have known better than to ride with him, but that money meant everything.

He lurched against me as we started out. "Wow, I feel like I'm flying," he said, and the car swerved and weaved back and forth down the deserted street. I recall feeling that this was madness—suicide even, that I should have him stop the car so I could get out.

Instead, I reached for his coat pocket and he lifted his hands off the wheel. What happened next took only a second or so, but in my condition it seemed to be slow motion. The car continued rolling, now out of control, for perhaps 200 feet before slamming into a light pole.

Several seconds after the impact, I came to, my face smashed against the dash. Searing pain had a sobering effect, and I was shivering. I alternated in and out of a dull consciousness, as excruciatingly sharp pains stabbed through my face and upper chest. I became aware of the smell of gasoline, and noticed the driver out cold against the wheel. Somehow I extricated myself from the wreck, and managed to free the driver before I collapsed.

I remember nothing of the next few minutes, but when I regained consciousness, I was in an ambulance, and voices that seemed to be coming from another room were fading in and out. I heard an attendant talking above the noise of sirens. "That fellow over there, he might make it, but this man doesn't have a chance. Look at his face—it's busted like an egg."

He must have thought I was unconscious, but for that moment my head was clear, and I perceived he was talking about me. I was experiencing intense pain in my face.

I could hear the attendants working to bring the driver in

next to me, as I tried touching my face. But I couldn't move my arms. Neither could I open my eyes. Or, if I did, I couldn't see.

There was only the indescribable pain. I tried to cry out, to make some sound, but nothing happened.

I thought to myself that this was the end. But I wasn't ready to die. Not yet. "I'm only 34," I told myself, "and I haven't lived yet."

Yet all I'd ever done was hurt others and waste myself. I couldn't think of one decent thing I'd done in my life. And I thought of how I had continually hurt Mom and my family. But there was nothing I could do about that now.

There are reports that a man's life passes before him in the last moments of life. And since this was now happening to me, I was sure death was at hand. At least this time, all those I had hurt would be rid of me forever.

But in a moment of lucidity—remarkable, considering my condition—I thought about God and where I was going. I knew about the reality of God and the consequences of going against Him. I was sure of the reality of hell, and knew that's where I'd be going.

I kept hearing a voice from the depths of what might have been delirium saying, "This is it, man. This is it. You're all through."

Then I was hearing the words of my Mom. "You can always call on the Lord and He will answer."

But the Satan part of me answered, "Ain't no use calling on God—you've been too bad. You ain't done nothing for Him, and He won't do nothing for you."

But I didn't want to die. I tried to form sounds with my lips but nothing came. I prayed silently, with more force and conviction than I ever had before. "Lord, let me live. Lord Jesus, please let me live. I don't want to die, Lord. Please let me live."

At that point I lapsed into oblivion again, away from pain and the reality of the moment. I was unconscious for two days, waking to find myself in a hospital bed.

I had been taken to General Hospital in Minneapolis in critical condition. Apparently I was given emergency attention upon my arrival, but doctors had given up hope for me, and had spent their time working on those who had a chance to pull through. Surgery was impossible for me because of all the drugs and booze in my system, so the only thing doctors were able to do for me was to stop the bleeding and try to keep me comfortable until the end came.

Off and on over the next three days I'd become conscious and aware of my surroundings. I also knew something was radically wrong. Though in acute pain, I occasionally moved or turned my head, and when I did, the inside of my mouth moved.

I later learned that the impact of the collision had forced my hard palate to split in the middle and break off at the side in a right angle. In effect, the entire roof of my mouth had broken loose, and it was that which flopped back and forth when I turned my head. In addition my nose was pushed completely into my face, leaving two orifices in the middle of what I used to consider a pretty goodlooking mug.

Doctors were amazed when I survived that first night, and even more amazed when I lived three days. By now, of course, the poisons I'd ingested had worked their way free of my system and some surgery was possible.

Miraculously, I had lost no teeth during the accident, and the team of surgeons was able to put what was left of my face back together with wires and sutures. They put my palate back in place except for a piece about the size of a dime. Whole operation took eight hours.

With my nose covered up, I had to breathe through a tracheotomy tube in my throat for the next two months. And with my mouth wired shut, I had to be fed intravenously.

During the days and weeks following surgery, I phased in and out of reality. But within a period of time, I began feeling stronger and grew more aware of what was going on.

I was confined to bed for seven weeks, but as I progressed, I was able to communicate with nurses and aides by writing notes on paper. Until then, however, I didn't know how badly I'd been hurt.

I discovered the extent of my injuries one day when I felt strong enough to roll the cart—with the intravenous tubes connected to it—along with me as I sneaked off to the bathroom for a cigarette. I didn't look in the mirror right off. I tried first to light the smoke. But to my surprise, I couldn't draw because of the cleft palate and the tube in my trachea.

It was then I looked in the mirror—and fell back in horror. I was less than human, a man without a face. I had always taken physical features for granted and thought I was God's gift to women and—as far as that goes—to the whole world. But now I had to look at myself without a face. In its place was a ghastly, gruesome mask.

There seemed no point in living now, and I decided I wasn't going to fight any more. I crept back to bed and wept.

Shortly after, a doctor came to see me, and I wrote on my pad, "I might as well be dead." I don't know if that doctor was a Christian or not, but he looked at me for a moment, and his eyes narrowed. I'd get no pity from this man.

"Let me tell you something," he began. "Every day of your life, you get down on your knees and thank God you're alive. You're not supposed to be here at all under any circumstances. None of us who operated on you has any idea how we got you together. But here you are.

"Ask us to do something like this tomorrow and we might not be able to. None of us had ever seen anything like you before, and we've seen some pretty hopeless cases. People in better shape than you have come in here and died in a couple of hours. But you lived.

"You thank God, because without Him we couldn't have done it. Your face was actually torn away from your head. Your life is a miracle."

And that miracle can best be proved by my appearance today. I have no scars from that accident, except for one small one beneath my right eye where a friend took a dirty razor and snipped some stitches prematurely when I was out of the hospital on leave. That later infected, and a tiny scar remains. Otherwise my skin is smooth.

Though I wasn't thanking God for saving me, I decided then I wasn't going to quit on myself either. The doctors said future surgery might do something to give me a normal appearance, and I could live with that.

As time passed, I inquired about getting out of the hospital. But the staff informed me that was impossible for a while, because I couldn't eat food. I was told to have patience and be thankful I was alive at all.

The day after I'd been told that no definite time could be set for my release, my landlord, George Warren, came to the hospital. He asked for me as Buddy Jefferson, but since I was registered under Arnold Jefferson, he was told there was no one by that name in the hospital. When he described my condition, they said he could look for me if he wanted.

George had come because someone had told him I was in the hospital dying, and this fine Christian was determined I wouldn't die without his giving me at least one more testimony. How I thank God for him.

Now this was a man in his seventies, a man who had not acquired material goods in his lifetime, an able, gifted man who could have been bitter about the racial animosities that had kept him from reaching his full worldly potential. But all he thought about then was to bring the Lord Jesus to Ted Jefferson.

After nearly two hours of wandering up and down the wards in that massive metropolitan hospital, he found me. I was dozing when he approached my bed and took my hand.

"Buddy, Buddy," he whispered.

I turned to gaze at his grizzled, kindly face. And despite the atmosphere of pain, sickness and death, I could truly see the light of Jesus Christ in his eyes. As he bent over me, I felt just a tug of pity for this man whom I had ripped off for different small articles on occasion.

"Buddy, do you believe God can have you out of here by Sunday?"

After a pause, I nodded.

"Then I'll be back here with your clothes on Sunday," he said and quietly left.

The next day I began feeling stronger. To the amazement of the staff, I started walking around, visiting other patients and encouraging them. On my note pad, I wrote the doctors that I would be going home on Sunday and said they had to help me to eat.

Minor surgery cut loose two molars, and since my jaw was still wired shut, I was given a syringe-like device, with which I could force soups and soft foods back into my mouth for nourishment.

George came back on Sunday with some clothes. He related some sad news too—my room had been burglarized, and I had no shirts. He hadn't thought to bring an extra one, but right there in my room he took off his own and put it on me, then buttoned up his suit coat and led me from the ward.

No doctor would sign my release; I had to do that myself and waive responsibility. But George said that since God got me out, God wasn't going to let me down now. I may not yet have had faith in the Lord, but I had faith in George's convictions and believed him.

Before I was discharged, however, I was cautioned against drinking. "If you drink and throw up, Arnold," I was told, "you could drown. Your mouth is still wired shut and will be for some time."

I promised I wouldn't drink. But in my life, promises were made to be broken.

Ted Jefferson and his sister, Corrine, stand outside the ramshackle log cabin in Wisconsin's Butler Township where Ted was born on December 7, 1932.

Theodore and Verbena Jefferson, Ted's parents, with his sister, Corrine. Photographed in 1932

Ted at about age four with Corrine and aunts and uncles in Stanley, Wisconsin. Ted is front row, right.

Ted with Jimmy Larson, who did time for drug-related crimes and who now serves as assistant director of Fair Haven Christian Household, heads up the organization's expanding ministry to youth.

Ted with the Rev. Richard Knowles, head chaplain of the Minnesota State Prison at Stillwater.

Cary H. Humphries, vice-president of Cargill, Inc., first met Ted through Amicus, Inc., when Ted was still in Minnesota State Prison at Stillwater. Cary is now a member of the Fair Haven Board of Directors.

Ted, as a member of the prison chaplain's staff at Stillwater, counsels Gregory Demmings, an inmate.

The Jefferson family (1978). Front row (l. to r.)—Yvonne, Marie, Deborah. Back row (l. to r.)—Ted, Kelvin, Yvette, Kerwin. (In separate photo) Carol.

Ted and Garmon Harrison, a lifelong friend, former brother-in-law and fellow evangelist. Photographed in 1949.

Ted (34) and Marie (27) Jefferson in September, 1967.

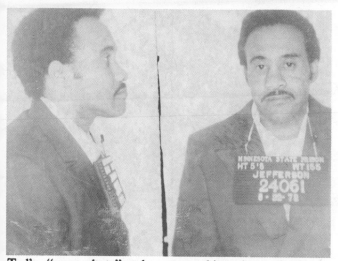

Ted's "mug shots" taken upon his release from the Minnesota State Prison at Stillwater, August 22, 1972.

Michael Fedo and Ted prayerfully plan their collaboration together on *One Bad Dude*.

Ted welcomes Kerwin, his once-estranged son from Milwaukee, home to the family in Minneapolis.

The Fair Haven Christian Household, an evangelical halfway house for ex-convicts, established by Ted in 1975.

Ted with Karl Kassulke, former defensive back for the
Minnesota Vikings, shared the podium at a recent Amicus
banquet in the Minnesota State Prison at Stillwater.

Ted preaches in revival services held at
Southern University A&M, Baton Rouge,
Louisiana, 1977.

State of Minnesota

DEPARTMENT OF CORRECTIONS

MINNESOTA CORRECTIONS AUTHORITY

To Theodore Jefferson
Parolee - Inmate

24061

At a regular meeting of the Minnesota Corrections Authority, held August 27, 1976 *the discharge of* Theodore Jefferson *No.* 24061, *an inmate at the Minnesota State* Prison Stillwater, *Minnesota, was authorized to take effect* August 27, 1976, *and he is hereby restored to all civil rights and to full citizenship, with full right to vote and hold office, the same as if such conviction had not taken place.*

MINNESOTA CORRECTIONS AUTHORITY

Corr. 260 (7-74)

Hallelujah!

I cried when I got this. For once in my life I was completely free.

No parole officer, no probation officer, no police or F.B.I. looking for me.

"If the Son therefore shall make you free, you shall be free indeed."

Praise God! Thank You Jesus!

Chapter 8

TAKING A LIFE

I shot up the office, demanding my check.

Once free of the hospital, I quickly ignored ordinary precautions concerning my health. The second day out, I started swilling wine, though fortunately I didn't get sick.

I thought I could do whatever I wanted to now, and while I should have been thankful that my strength was returning, I was indulging in self-pity for my appearance and my distorted cleft-palate speech.

Despite the warm Christian overtures of George Warren, I was right back to drinking and gambling. But George kept at me to call my wife. Filled with guilt over abandoning her, I refused, until one day I did phone Mom in Milwaukee, and Marie was at her house. I was forced into speaking to her and feared the worst. But all she said was, "When are you coming to get me?"

No accusations or threats. Marie never asked why I'd done this to her and the kids. She said only that she missed me and wanted to be with me.

I tried to explain that I wasn't the same—I had no job, no money. I didn't look like the man I'd been, and I certainly didn't sound like him. But that made no difference to Marie. The family should be together she said. Before hanging up, I said I'd do what I could.

That night I prayed that God would find me a job in Minneapolis so I could send for my family. Later that week my teeth were cut loose and I was able to open my mouth. My speech was not improved, however, and I still had some wires in my head—clamps holding other portions of my facial bones together.

The next morning I went to a bucket factory on Fifth Street and entered the office. The effects of a dozen major operations coupled with my inability to articulate must have caused the owner to look at me as some sort of freak. He probably thought I'd recently escaped from some hospital.

I made him understand that I was applying for a job, but he shook his head. "I can't give you a job."

"You're going to give me a job," I persisted.

He swallowed hard. "No, I won't give you a job."

"You'll give me work." I was amazed at my forcefulness.

He shook his head and sat down. "What makes you think I'll give you a job?"

"I just know you will. I'll work hard for you. I've prayed about this and you'll give me a job."

I then explained that I had to get my wife from Milwaukee and told him that somebody had to help me. "I'm walking past this place every day back and forth from the hospital. I have no money. I never thought about it before, but today I came in here knowing you were going to give me work."

He shook his head again, looked at me, then shook his head. "You're crazy. How can I hire you? You can't talk—nobody can understand you."

He stared at me, while inside I was praying, "Lord, I need this job. Help me Lord Jesus."

He banged his fist down on his cluttered desk. "Okay, anybody that comes in here like this, in your condition, has to have guts. You just might be okay. I'll start you off at $1.75 an hour, but you have to promise you'll stay with me a year. I'll want you working here after you get well."

I promised, and he told me he wouldn't have me work in the yard, but would let me take it easy in the office until I was fully recovered. Two weeks later, this Jewish man loaned me $100 so I could bring my family to Minneapolis.

Some friends and I rented a truck and, in the wee hours of the morning, spirited my family to the train depot, where we boarded the train for the Twin Cities, while my friends loaded our furniture in the truck. The operation had to be secret, because I was still wanted in Wisconsin for parole violation. I had left the state without clearing it with my agent, and there were nonsupport warrants out for me also.

Now after a four-month absence, we were all together again, in a small apartment on the north side of town. Marie thanked the Lord for my safety and praised Him for allowing us to be a family once more.

We started attending church in St. Paul, and though I was again serious about religion, I really never thought I would change deep down in my heart. I was a hypocrite, going to church on Sunday and living a worldly life from Monday through Saturday.

The sad part of this episode is that so many people had hopes for me. I recovered nicely from my accident, until all that remained was that cleft-palate speech. Several subsequent operations to close the cleft had failed, but despite this handicap, I was able to speak with conviction, giving a number of testimonies in our church.

Some of the older members used to say admiringly, "This young man is going to be a preacher. He's going to do great works for the Lord. God certainly has His hand upon him."

I used to hate hearing them say that because I knew my heart wasn't right with God. And there was torment inside me because I knew I wasn't like these fine folks who trusted me and who encouraged me in the ways of the Lord.

I didn't want to find myself under this pressure any longer, so finally I simply stopped attending church, and returned with gusto to my drinking and doping habits. Within a few weeks it was plain for all to see that there was no change whatsoever in Ted Jefferson.

The bottom dropped out one day in late November. Our year-old daughter, Sherry, was already running a low-grade fever when I took off on a gambling spree for several days. When I finally got back home again, I found the house cold and drafty, Marie sick in bed and Sherry asleep.

I asked our oldest daughter how long the baby had been sleeping. She told me the little one had not stirred for two or three hours. I felt that was too long for her to sleep in the middle of the day, so I went to Sherry's room and checked her.

I found the baby lying there, not asleep, but listless and burning with fever. I knew Sherry was seriously ill. And right there I prayed that the Lord would have mercy.

I didn't feel right in praying then, knowing I wasn't right with the Lord. But, as was my habit when things looked grim, I'd simply cast a prayer out in the great somewhere hoping God might pick it up.

We brought the baby to General Hospital where she lapsed into a coma. Doctors told me she was going to die, but didn't tell Marie. I couldn't bring myself to tell her either, and it broke me up to see her pacing back and forth in the corridor, praying and holding out hope for recovery.

Miracles had happened before, but this time, I felt there'd be no miracle. God is not mocked. And I was without faith.

When Sherry died three days later, I got mad, got drunk and blamed God for the loss. In my rage, I cried out, "If You wanted to kill someone, why didn't You kill me?"

My anger against God eventually subsided, and I put the blame where it belonged—on my own shoulders. If I had been taking care of the family, maybe this wouldn't have happened, I told myself.

Sure, I had kept my job at the bucket factory, but that was out of the goodness of the owner, who didn't fire me when I would come in late, drunk or high on drugs—or wouldn't show up at all. He told me I was a good worker when not drinking or doping, and he tried to get me into recovery programs. But instead of repaying him for his genuine concern, I went to him after Sherry's funeral and quit. I had a pistol and shot up his office, demanding my check.

He wrote it out, more hurt than disgusted, and he said as he handed it to me, "Don't you ever come back here again."

I took the money, blew it on booze and drugs and stayed high for several weeks—weeks I no longer remember. Even now they leave a blank space in my mind.

I don't remember the particulars, but I evidently returned to my employer and apologized, and the man took me back. "Arnold," he said. "If you're not drinking, you're one of the best men I've got. I want to help you because you can work—you're not like these other bums who come in here and work for a day or two. Maybe you should get into AA and see if you can't bring this under control."

I agreed to anything, so long as I could keep my old job. I knew that at 36 I had to pull myself together, or for sure it wouldn't be long before I'd be back in the slammer. This time somebody would throw away the key, and nobody, but nobody would care.

I worked hard for three weeks and never missed a day. Then one afternoon I took off and got drunk, sneaking back at four o'clock to change my clothes. The boss said nothing, so I figured maybe he hadn't noticed.

This errant behavior was rewarded, however, and I was made yard foreman and got a raise in pay. The boss also bought me some good furniture for my family and made numerous attempts to help me get my personal life squared away. He often said that I had the ability to run the yard for him, except for my drinking. I still thought I could cure myself, so I went out and obtained a second job as a welder. In between jobs I stayed high, but didn't think I had a bad problem because I still managed to work.

My own self-remedy consisted of staying off drink and dope during the week and letting go on weekends. I was like a diseased plant when the florist snips the impaired growth but leaves the bad roots untouched. I couldn't rid myself of those bad roots.

Then one Friday just before Christmas, I received two paychecks—one from each job. I stopped in a bar to cash

101

the checks and was only going to have a few drinks before heading home. But for a confirmed alcoholic like me, those few drinks soon became many. I began bar-hopping before 7 p.m. and was still at it long after midnight, with no thought at all for my family who waited for me to come home with the money.

After the saloons closed for the night, I continued my binge in sleazy after-hour joints. First thing I knew, it was Saturday morning and I was broke. I knew I couldn't go home like that; I had to get some money. I met another fellow with a pistol and we started pulling a series of street crimes for more money—$50 here, $25 there. But instead of pocketing it, we blew it on more booze.

I was totally out of control now, riding a roller coaster I couldn't get off. Whenever the edge of the alcoholic haze would clear, I'd realize that I was throwing everything away and something inside me would scream out to stop. But then some acquaintance would place another bottle before me, and once again the warning would be ignored.

Looking back on this time of my life is like remembering a bad dream. It doesn't seem possible to have lived it, let alone to have dreamed it. For some reason, my buddy and I kidnapped a man and kept him locked in a closet at a friend's apartment for a couple of days.

I don't remember why we took the man, except I used his identification to purchase another pistol of my own. Even then, I knew there was only one reason for me to own a weapon. I would use it in the commission of crimes.

Fortunately, the man never reported his abduction; he may have been too drunk to remember it. For even after we released him, he stayed with us and shared our liquor until that too was gone.

The squalid horror continued through another day and another. Every time we'd pull a robbery I'd tell myself it was time to go home. But instead of returning home, I'd reach for more booze, more pot, more pills and stay high, oblivious to the doom that waited around the corner for me.

Satan had determined this time there'd be no going

home for me. I was hopelessly snared in his trap, and his voice reinforced my belief that now, this time I'd surely stepped over the brink and beyond God's forgiveness. I seemed to have forgotten all the promises of God's Word.

Eventually, all of us got too high to continue boosting. So we decided to go home—home, that is to an after-hours joint where we usually hung out. And there we spent the night drinking our booze, counting our loot and smoking pot.

Then in the early morning, another dude whom I recognized as a former friend came in with some of his gambling buddies. I watched him walk through the door and felt my hackles rise. For though I had never admitted it to myself or anyone else, I genuinely hated this man.

You know, sin isn't always conceived on the spot. Sometimes it just festers and grows and seethes inside a person, as had my degenerate, spiteful feelings toward this man.

Even though we knew each other and even went on sprees together, we'd often argue. And I recall telling myself that if he kept pushing me, I'd kill him—just blow him away.

It had all started many months earlier when he made an obscene remark to my wife. It had shaken her, and when she told me about it, I said, "I'm going to kill that dude."

"No—no," Marie said in panic. "You'll only get into more trouble."

Though I kept telling myself I'd do it, I never intended to kill him—not really. But that Wednesday—Christmas Eve, 1969—all the old feeling of hate for him just boiled up inside me, until I was standing up, repeatedly pulling the trigger on my revolver and realizing that indeed, I had killed him.

I had taken a human life.

The escape route took me first to Milwaukee, where I had to visit my Mom. She sensed my unrest and agitation and finally I had to tell her, "Ma, I've killed a man."

She gasped and turned ashen. "No—no—," she moaned, as she broke down and wept. I had some feeling

103

for her then, knowing that she'd been praying and fasting and sacrificing for me all these years, hoping and trusting that I'd come to the true Savior and would trust Him too.

She refused to believe that I could have gotten myself so completely messed up. And though I didn't know it then, she was also praying silently that the Lord would slow down the rapid beating of her heart. During the last months, she had developed a grave heart condition that I wasn't aware of. The shock of my announcement led her to think she was on the verge of a heart attack.

"It's true, Ma," I said again. "What should I do?"

Through her deep misery and tears, she tried to convince me to give myself up.

"But Ma, with my record, that means life in prison. I don't want to go to jail for the rest of my life. And I'm not going to. There's no way I will rot in That Man's jail."

The only thing left for me to do was split. Get out of town. And the sooner the better.

Before I left Milwaukee though, I visited an old friend from my street days. Anything to keep my mind occupied. I hardly recognized the man. Totally strung out on drugs, he looked like a breathing skeleton. We reminisced a while about the old days and how everyone from the old gang was either dead, in the joint, on the lam or strung out.

"We've all made a pretty good mess of things, ain't we?" I said, before leaving.

"Yes, man," answered my friend. "We sure goofed. All the plans we made, we sure blew the whole thing."

There was nothing left for me in Milwaukee then. And I wondered if there was any place, anywhere, where Ted Jefferson could hide and forget—start over and forget.

I decided I'd go and stay for a while with an aunt in Chicago. But my being there proved too much pressure for her. So I moved on to Detroit, where there were people I'd done time with who might hide me.

My Detroit connection dealt in drugs, and he agreed to help me. He helped me all right. He got me hooked on the hard stuff.

Nights became sheer torture for me. My mind seemed

turned in directly to Satan. "Buddy, you are dead, man. It's all over for you now. You killed that man. You killed him. Look at him. Look at the blood.

"You did this, Buddy, and now you must suffer. Look at his face. See his pain. You will die too."

Thrashing in my sleep, I'd think, "I'm going to die. I'm going to die."

But I couldn't die now. I hadn't lived yet. I couldn't stand the thought of dying, and there seemed only one way to escape it. I'd have to get high—and higher.

Chapter 9
FINDING IT'S REAL

"Hey, man. Why'd you
throw my mattress out?"

Within a few weeks, I realized that I was getting a habit my Detroit friend wasn't likely to continue supporting. And sure enough, he soon evicted me. But by then I had found a job in a car wash which enabled me to afford a flophouse room and booze or occasional drugs.

But Detroit is a mean city, even for a dude like me. One day a group of unfamiliar brothers hailed me on the street, offering to share a bottle of gin. A friendly face, a kind word was just what I needed then, so I joined them. But as the bottle passed to me, they nailed me. The lights went out, and I came to some time later, abandoned and bleeding on a sub-freezing street in the Detroit ghetto.

I was badly done in and for no reason, save the cheap sadistic thrill that deranged minds find fulfilling when hurting others. I could understand it if they'd hit me for money, but I had nothing.

The thing that really threw me was that I didn't know those dudes and had never seen them before. They had beaten me just for the thrill of it.

Fearing the FBI had already put out a wanted poster on me, I couldn't go to a hospital. So I nursed my broken nose and bruises and cuts in my room for three days with a bottle of cheap wine.

Two other acquaintances were wanted in Columbus and Chicago, and we had an informal arrangement to look out for each other. And what little money we had, we pooled.

So we survived. But was that what life was all about? Just surviving from day to day in the most miserable conditions?

While in Detroit, I'd phone Marie every few weeks just to let her know I was still alive. Usually I'd jive her, tell her that things would be cool and we'd soon get out of this mess. But she was no fool;she knew a man couldn't dodge a murder rap indefinitely.

I knew that too, and finally one night when I was in a tavern, I stumbled to the pay phone and rang her again. "Look," I said. "It's all over. No games anymore. I love you, but I'm never coming back to face that life sentence. If I went back, I wouldn't have you and the kids anyway.

"They're going to have to kill me before I go back. Forget me. You'll never see me again."

Marie was crushed. She cried and slid down to the floor, sobbing uncontrollably. I hung up. Later she would tell me that she believed her world ended with that phone call.

My wife was a shy woman and had not made friends easily. Her life centered around her home and family. And now even that was crumbling and falling away from her.

But finally, when Marie had caught her breath, she could think of only one thing to do. She began to pray that God would take away her awful hurt. She prayed for nearly an hour, then got up and went to bed.

When she woke next morning, she felt better. God had given her strength to endure. Now she did not feel sorry for herself any more, for the Lord would help her survive.

But me? I was depressed. I couldn't go back and face a charge of murder one. So I wandered the city aimlessly.

A few days later, shivering from cold and trying to ward off the chill, I stopped in a little rescue mission. The preacher was laying it on pretty heavily. When a man is guilty of something and a preacher starts zeroing in on it, he thinks the speaker is talking directly to him.

So, as I sat there, I felt this old preacher was starting in on me. His eyes seemed riveted on me and his words

directed at me, as if I was the only one there in that whole crowd of bums and derelicts.

"I know maybe you've left your wife and kids. Maybe you've done some horrible crime, but Jesus loves you," the preacher explained. He quoted John 10:9. "Jesus said. *I am the door: by Me if any man enter in, he shall be saved.*"

I was beginning to seat in that damp, cold mission. But the preacher pressed his point. "The Lord says, 'Any man can come.' And 'any man' means boy, brother, black man, police man, government man—any man at all."

The Holy Spirit was pulling me. I wanted to cry out, "Lord, I can't handle it any more." So while I sat there, I prayed, "Lord, I ain't got the nerve to go forward. But if You help me, I want to go back to Minneapolis. I'm all tired out, but You take care of it."

God did want me back in Minneapolis. And He was already taking care of it. The night before my encounter at the mission, two detectives stopped several of us outside an after-hours joint. One asked for my identification, and I gave it to him.

Though they eventually let us go, one of the officers kept staring at me. Later, when this same officer was almost ready to go off his shift, he told his partner, "There's something about that guy." He looked at a recent FBI flyer and traced me down through my social security number which—though under a false name—led them to the car wash.

Three days after the Lord began dealing with me in that mission, FBI agents came into the car wash where I was working and said, "Arnold Jefferson, come on. You're wanted back in Minneapolis for the charge of first degree murder."

My stomach churned, but I kept my outward cool. I wanted to act tough for the other guys there. But inside I was glad, because now it was over with. I was through running and through fighting.

I was taken to the Wayne County Jail, where I was accidentally thrown in with the younger inmates, instead of with men my own age. Though only there a few weeks, I can say in all honesty that in all my life this was the worst place I'd ever been in. I was sickened by the sights and sounds of blatant homosexual rapes of young men who may have been jailed for the first time.

Within a few days jail officials discovered I was 37 and placed me then with the roughest bunch of thugs I'd ever seen. The entire attitude of those inmates was of rage and hatred. There were men awaiting extradition into southern states where murders and rapes had been committed. Since they figured it would be easier to do time in a northern prison, they openly talked about killing some weaker inmate. Though this didn't happen while I was there, I have no doubt that some of these men were capable of the most cruel and inhuman acts imaginable.

The physical plant itself was disgraceful. There were roaches in the shower. And the cells, designed for two inmates each, were packed with three or four men. There wasn't a moment when any but the biggest and strongest of men could feel safe.

I wasn't assigned to a cell there; just given a thin mattress and told to find a spot. I found one with only one bottom bunk occupied, so I assumed it would be the place for me and claimed the upper bunk.

I didn't know at the time that the upper bunk was taken by a big black dude, standing six-feet-six, with a massive girth. When he came in he cursed me for stepping into "his" cell, and he threw my mattress into the hall. The others gathered around, anticipating some action, wondering how five-foot-nine-inch Ted, would cope, with this bruiser.

A man must never show weakness in prison. So though never doubting this man could tear me apart, I had to stand up for myself. I had to let him think that, though he might take me, it might not be worth the effort.

Careful not to allow a fearful or belligerent edge to creep into my voice, I said simply, "Hey, man, why'd you throw my mattress out? I have to sleep somewhere."

It took him back. No one had ever stood up to him,

before. And while he didn't back down, he did point out another spot for me to sleep on, adding that I'd better stay out of his way from now on. The fact that he didn't fight me probably gave me status among other inmates. And thank the Lord, I was personally left alone by the men in there. I could breathe easier now.

While in that cramped cell, I managed to find a copy of David Wilkerson's book, *The Cross and the Switchblade.* And the story of this white man going into that ghetto, sleeping in his car, trusting the Lord would protect him, deeply touched me. For the first time since childhood, tough Ted Jefferson broke down and sobbed.

The book gave me a lift, and I said to myself, "If the Lord can take care of that man, He'll take care of me too." And I felt everything would be all right.

I began praying in my cell, calling on the Lord to extend His mercy to me and to give me the strength I'd need to face up to the hideous crime I'd committed. I'd gone to God before when faced with big trouble, but I'd always let Him and myself down. This time, I felt it would be different, though I really had not yet opened my heart.

I guess I needed proof, a sign, a miracle before I could seriously turn over my life. That's why what I was feeling was so important. It meant that I was probably ready to receive Christ, that I was really serious about looking for salvation at last.

I wrote Marie and told her I was looking to God to see me through. Somehow she believed I was sincere this time.

After I wrote Marie, I told officers there that I would waive extradition. And in a few days I was winging my way back to Minneapolis in the custody of one of that city's detectives. On arrival there, I was transferred to the Hennepin County Jail.

Marie came to visit me in the jail, and when we met, we both cried. We talked about what the Lord had done for us despite everything. We had been blessed with wonderful children and told ourselves that things would work out for the best.

A public defender was soon assigned to my case. And at

112

our first meeting, my court-appointed counsel was highly pessimistic. He had examined my record and offered no hope. "Ted, you just don't stand a chance." he said. "With your record, you can't expect anything. I'll do what I can for you, but I want you to understand that there doesn't look like much we can do."

He didn't come right out and say it, but I figured what he meant was I'd probably get the life sentence. So I pressed him. "What does that mean?" I asked.

He sighed. "Your're 37 now. I'll be honest with you. You can't figure on getting out until you're 54."

His words confirmed my suspicions. He was talking in terms of 17 years, and I already knew that most lifers are eligible for serious parole consideration after serving about 17 years of their sentences. He was telling me I'd get life.

Yet I could hardly comprehend a 17-year sentence in even the best run big house. I was still a young man, but I'd be old when I got out. My family, my children would be grown up and gone without ever really knowing me.

I didn't know what to think anymore. I was plain exhausted and a little confused. And I didn't want to burden anyone. Especially Marie. I just wanted to be left alone. I guess God in His tender mercy was breaking me down to where He could reach me.

It was at this time that Marie showed me her determination and grit. She had grown close to the Lord and constantly encouraged me, vowing she'd stick by me. She told me I wasn't going to receive a life sentence. She didn't know how it could be, but she was firmly convinced I wouldn't get life.

But what could she know? Marie'd never been through the criminal justice system. She was naive, only kidding herself and probably just trying to keep me from getting discouraged. And I figured when the realization of what happens to me finally hits her, she'd get discouraged herself, despite her faith.

So for Marie's sake, I tried to put on an optimistic front, but I knew what I was up against. Also, I had seen many other wives talk this same way when their husbands were sent to prison. "Honey, I'll wait forever. Don't worry, baby. Everything's gonna be all right. I'll be right here when you get out." Then before the man could change from civilian to prison clothes, they would be out with other men, having a ball. So I was sure if I received a life sentence, it would be all over for Marie and me. How little I understood her love and loyalty.

The doubt and uneasiness gnawed at my mind. Whom could I trust? I felt myself pulling away from the Lord, feeling that perhaps He was going to let that life sentence stand. I deserved it, but I didn't want it.

Maybe God wanted me to sweat for a while. But I didn't want to sweat. I didn't want to think, and I began moving slightly away from God. To while away the long empty hours in jail, I gambled with other prisoners.

Still, a part of me wanted Jesus, and in the evenings I resumed my old habit of turning to Him by reading the Bible and offering an occasional halfhearted prayer. I yet held out hope for a conviction of less than first degree murder, and hoped that God just might assist me in that regard.

I really hadn't counted on being spiritually moved by the power and glory of the Lord, until one night, my Bible opened to the fifty-first Psalm. There I read David's prayer for remission of sin. *Have mercy upon me, O God, according to thy loving kindness; according unto the multitude of thy tender mercies blot out my transgressions,* I read in the first verse. And further on in the tenth verse: *Create in me a clean heart, O God; and renew a right spirit within me.*

As I read and pondered the words, the Lord began to speak to me, asking me about the pain in my heart, the pain I'd caused all my life. He showed me how selfish I'd been—how my concern was always for myself with utter disregard for others. Even now, I was concerned about myself, about getting a light sentence. I felt no remorse for the killing of that man, no compassion for his parents. I was still tough Teddy, hoping that God would have mercy on me simply so I could have live a little easier.

But now in my cell, it was as if the Lord had stripped me naked, exposing to me all the falseness and wickedness that had been my whole life until this very moment. I decided that I wanted to be honest with God and with everybody.

I prayed, "God, make me into Your servant. I can't do it myself. You said you could create a new heart, that old things would be passed away. You do it. Help me, Lord. Help me. Help me to be the man You want me to be. Come into my heart right now."

I asked God to break me, tear me apart, give me that new heart and accept me into His kingdom. I simply asked Him, finally, to take over my entire life, every facet of it.

I felt like a small quivering rat as I lay there, ever so tiny in the sight of my God. I felt the tears rise into my eyes, rush past the lids and fall splashing to the cot. I had never cried like this before, as all the hurt, the pain, the loneliness and bitterness were washed away by the precious blood of Jesus. Wonderful Jesus. Bless His Holy Name!

Then suddenly it was as though a light filled my cell and I was on my feet, laughing, crying praying and praising the Lord. If anyone had seen me he would have thought I was stone crazy. I was being baptized by Jesus in His blessed Holy Spirit.

All my life I had known something was lacking in me. Even when I had tried to live a Christian life, I felt there was more—something beyond what I had. And now I knew what it was—the power of the baptism in the mighty Holy Ghost. John the Baptist preached to the people, *I indeed baptize you with water unto repentance: but he that cometh after me is mightier than I, whose shoes I am not worthy to bear: he shall baptize you with the Holy Ghost, and with fire* (Matthew 3:11).

And Jesus Himself said, *For John truly baptized with water; but ye shall be baptized with the Holy Ghost not many days hence. . .*

But ye shall receive power, after that the Holy Ghost is come upon you: and ye shall be witnesses unto me both in

Jerusalem, and in all Judaea, and in Samaria, and unto the uttermost part of the earth (Acts 1:5, 8).

And now, praise God, that experience was mine. So much was happening to me in that cell that describing it at all is difficult. But I remember how wave upon wave of pure joy rushed through me and over me, as I was engulfed in the divine and indescribable love and presence of Jesus Christ.

Suddenly Jesus' name took on a new and tremendous meaning for me. He truly is the Son of God. This is Jesus who shed His blood for me, was beaten for me, was reviled by man and was spat upon for me, and who allowed Himself to be nailed to the cross to die for me.

There I was, 37 years old, but a brand-new babe in Christ—born again at last of the Spirit of God. And there in the cell, a Scripture verse came into mind. It was Galations 2:20 where Paul says, *I am crucified with Christ: nevertheless I live; yet not I but Christ liveth in me: and the life which I now live in the flesh I live by the faith of the Son of God, who loved me, and gave himself for me.*

I knew Ted Jefferson had died that night. From now on, it would indeed be Christ living in me.

Chapter **10**

PRAISING IN PRISON

"Buddy! It's real — it's real!"
she shouted over and
over again.

The day after my conversion when my cronies asked if I wanted to deal the cards, I said, "No," and told them of my encounter with Christ the night before. Nobody believed me for quite a while; they all thought I was putting on an act to impress the court. But even when they were finally convinced of my sincerity, all but one man laughed and told me I'd flipped.

But that one man, also awaiting trial for murder, said, "Ted, I'm happy for you. You've got something to hang onto.

"Yes, man," I told him. "I've got Jesus." I tried then to convince him further of God's love and mercy. Though he didn't accept the Lord, I continue praying for him as he serves his lengthy sentence at Stillwater.

That same afternoon, my lawyer came back to see me. He seemed quite cheerful in comparison with our first gloomy meeting. And with good reason. This lawyer, a public defender with a heavy case load, took time to conduct a thorough investigation of my background on his own time. He talked with my acquaintances, family, old employers and anybody else who might have known me.

"When we first talked, Ted, I saw something in you. I don't know exactly what, but I thought you were a guy worth saving."

He broke into a wide smile. "The good news is they've agreed to reduce the charge against you from first-degree murder to first-degree manslaughter. If you plead guilty you'll get 15 years."

Elated, I asked him how he'd managed to get the reduction.

"I believed you must have been provoked into that killing. You're not the kind of person to have simply shot a man down like that unless you felt threatened or were goaded."

Never again would I doubt the power of the Lord or the way He works all things to His honor and glory. I believe God led my lawyer to his investigation and subsequent conclusion, for it is highly unusual for an overworked public defender to undertake so extensive an investigation.

I returned to my cell, praising God for His mercy and vowing that I'd serve Him no matter what I'd have to endure in prison. For even in the confines of prison, I could be free. I could be free, because I knew—and others would soon know—that God was alive within me.

When I arrived at Stillwater, I was assigned to A block—the cell block housing most of the hardened cons. But that was to be expected. After all, a four-time loser like myself could hardly anticipate immediate assignment to the honor block.

Prison talk centers on sex and dope and scores and deals or on becoming a more elusive criminal when a man gets released. So I was soon wanting for conversation. I required spiritual food.

Imagine then my joy in meeting Maury Nygard at Stillwater. Maury was a prison worker who volunteered to conduct Bible study and worship services for inmates. I quickly joined his group in regular prayer and study meetings.

It wasn't the size of the group that impressed me. For they were small in number, only five. But the Holy Spirit worked mightily within them. These were tough, embittered men who had received the salvation of Jesus Christ, and whose very beings radiated the presence of the Holy Spirit.

We met in an open area off a main corridor. Other

119

inmates would come by and hear us praying and praising God. Some of the curious stopped to see what was going on. And while a few may have come to scoff and laugh, more came to find out what it was we had going.

The power of the Lord lured men back several times, and desperate souls became saved. So our group began to grow, and we nurtured each other in the Word of God.

At one time, eight of us in that group had collective time of 400 years over our heads. Totally down and out, we had nothing but the Lord. But in the Lord Jesus, we had everything.

While prison life is never pleasant, I knew that with Jesus, I could be happy in spite of adversity. And for me adversity was quick in coming.

I knew the Lord never promised any of us a rose garden here on earth. And Stillwater was sure no rose garden. So, as I turned my life over to Him in that prison, difficulties soon arose.

Much of that difficulty had to do with the social isolation I experienced at first. For the most part during the early months of my confinement, I couldn't always be in the company of the other Christians. And the non-Christians there just weren't all that excited about having me around. It wasn't hard to understand why.

The Muslim movement was strong among the black inmates, and, as far as I knw then, I was the only black Christian around. So I had to endure constant taunts from some of the black brothers. My turning to Christianity was to them a symbol of weakness, of my wanting to please white folks. That made me an outcast to some of the blacks.

And, as a black man, I had no standing with most white inmates either. So, for a while, except for my Christian friends, I was practically cut off from inmate society.

A committed Christian is the natural enemy of Satan, and Satan is cunning and clever. He does his best to throw stumbling blocks in the paths of new converts. I was no exception. There were numerous threats against me because of my beliefs. Most still thought I was a Christian only so I could get time off for good behavior by getting tight with the administration and guards.

Yet while some Christians might get beaten or have their cells ransacked, neither I nor my cell was ever touched. I trusted the Lord to look after me and my personal belongings, though many times my black brothers, upon seeing the poster of Jesus I had in my cell, would threaten to "tear down the white man's Jesus."

Taunts would come heavy too, when in the evenings I'd have to walk down the block with my Bible on my way to Bible class. Some of those cons could get pretty vicious. But I'd smile through the tenseness I'd feel in my guts and say, "Hallelujah! Praise the Lord."

Though locked up each night in my cell, I knew a rich freedom unfamiliar to me in the past. Every other time, when incarcerated, I'd do my time, trying to stay high so I wouldn't be bothered with my problems with wives, girl friends, kids or money. Now I was high on Christ and didn't worry about my problems. My thoughts were on Jesus, and I let Him take my worrries.

I could praise Him too, because of His goodness and mercies to me and my family. For, while I was in prison, Marie was taking the children to church, and trying to lead them in the Christian walk. But the housing project where they lived was a breeding ground for pimps, prostitutes and gamblers, and our oldest daughter was reaching the age when some of those slick dudes would be forcing their attentions on her. I knew that for certain; I used to be one of them.

But our family prayed about this problem, and soon after my three girls were saved. This was an enormous relief for me, because if they had gone the wrong way while I was away, I would have blamed myself for their fall and would have had a hard time forgiving myself. So when they received Christ, I no longer had to worry about how they would turn out.

Meanwhile, so hungry was I for knowledge of the Word, that I enrolled in nearly a dozen correspondence courses sponsored by many denominations. They all confirmed

122

one thing: that Jesus Christ is the way to salvation.

During those first months in prison, I witnessed wherever I could, whenever I could. And I met with almost universal hostility. Yet each morning I'd begin on my knees with this prayer: "Lord, give me a soul today. Give me one soul for my witness that he might be added to Your kingdom.

I witnessed to everybody—cellmates, workers, guards, secretaries—anyone I could buttonhole. And men who'd laughed at religion, who'd denied the Lord, were starting to turn to Him. There in the company of a solid band of convict Christians, there rose a mini-revival.

As men accepted Christ, they found eager, active support. There still were times when a Christian would walk down the halls and be cursed or threatened. But he'd call out, "Praise the Lord," and any Christian within hearing distance would echo his "Praise the Lord."

It was a beautiful and forceful witness for all of us, as the Christians moved down those hate-ridden corridors and were able to look upon their brothers, not with hate, but with love and praise for the Lord.

About this time, one of the most powerful scenes of Christian testimony I'd ever witnessed occurred there in the halls of that prison. And it happened one night, all because a fellow Christian brother had placed tracts on top of the toilet paper in the bathroom stalls.

Among the inmates was the cruelest, most vicious man I'd met yet. He was a man who had maimed people merely for the joy of hearing their bones crack. He had cut people just for the sadistic pleasure it gave him.

This formidable man picked up one of the tracts and read it. He came out a few minutes later, obviously disturbed, his face twisted and contorted. He grabbed my friend and pulled him toward him. My Christian brother's heart must have thundered in his throat.

"If this thing is real," the bully snarled, "and what you've been saying is true, then I want it.

"Brother, let's pray," my friend said.

And that tough man accepted Jesus Christ in the prison

bathroom. His face shone like a newborn baby's, for he was touched by the Holy Spirit. From then on, because of this new convert, the taunting of Christians diminished in Stillwater.

If there can be such things as warm and rewarding experiences in prison, I enjoyed the first time at Stillwater that my mother visited me there after I became a Christian. She hadn't seen me since the time I'd come through Milwaukee with the awful news that I'd killed a man. But she had since learned of my conversion through Marie's letters. And now after some weeks of scrimping and saving she had managed to scrape together enough money for a round-trip bus ticket so she could come and visit me.

Mom had been praying for me nearly 40 years, and now when her prayers seemed to be fulfilled, she had come to see God's answer for herself. Though she wanted to believe, she also knew the old Ted too well. She knew I could con people and she may have harbored fears that I was up to that old game again.

I knew Ma was coming and was nervous about it. It would be an emotional reunion, and I didn't want to cry in front of all the other inmates and visitors in the prison lounge. Finally, my name was called, and I was brought to the visitor's room.

I saw Ma come in. She didn't notice me right away, but as I started toward her, she stopped in her tracks and a huge smile swept across her face as we rushed for each other. "Buddy! It's real—it's real!" she shouted over and over as we hugged each other and wept.

At that moment I didn't care who saw me cry; I was thrilled to see my mother and to know that, for the first time in my life, I had done something that pleased her.

The visit also meant a great deal to Mom. She had been slowing down at home and was beginning to feel old. But after seeing me, she returned to Milwaukee and got a job in a nursing home where she started a vibrant witness among the old folks there. One time, while she giving an old man his bath, she led him to the Lord and baptized him right then and there in the tub.

Thank the Lord for the strength and faith of a Christian mother.

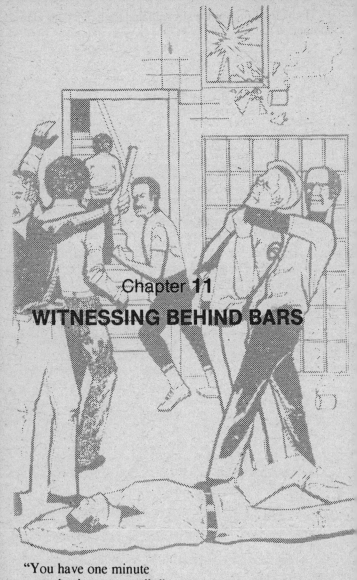

Chapter **11**

WITNESSING BEHIND BARS

"You have one minute
to get back to your cells."

As is the case with all inmates in Minnesota institutions, I went up before the parole board in four months, somehow thinking that I'd get out, even though logic dictated the impossibility of that. My discharge date was 1980, but there was a chance that with a good break, I might get out in seven years, in 1976.

I was turned down, but I went back to my cell praising God. I was not depressed. I was learning to accept what God wanted for me. There was a reason why God wanted me to stay in that prison, and I could accept His Word and His wishes. The board continued me for three years, and I'd have to wait that long for another review.

When I returned to my job, there were those who ribbed me. "Man, why didn't your Jesus get you out of here? You told us your God can do anything but fail, man. What do you call this—success?

I refused to be sucked into an argument, so I just smiled and said, "Well, that's okay. I got continued three years. But if I were a betting man, I'd bet I don't do the whole three years."

The guys burst into raucous laughter. "Man, you crazy. You are a jive turkey."

"Keep talking about that Jesus thing, and you'll never get out."

With quiet confidence I was able to speak, somehow feeling the assurance the Lord was supporting what I was about to say. "They're going to let me out of here on a special parole."

More hoots and laughter. "They don't let no man out of here on specials for no first-degree manslaughter," a man shouted derisively. "This cat's done blew his lid."

"Then I'll be the first one," I replied. "Mark my words, God will get me out of here on a special parole before the three years are up."

Problems and confrontations continued in the prison despite the growing number of Christians. But the teasing was easing off. I could sense the change in the men, as the Holy Spirit was at work, preparing the souls of these lost convicts.

Though I'd often abused my body in the past, one evening while reading my Bible, God spoke to me through His Word regarding this matter: *What? know ye not that your body is the temple of the Holy Ghost which is in you, which ye have of God, and ye are not your own? For ye are bought with a price: therefore glorify God in your body and in your spirit, which are God's* (I Corinthians 6:19-20).

I realized then that my body is a gift from God, and that I should honor it as if it were a holy temple. And I understood this to mean that I should refrain from physically or sexually abusing my body. So to relieve the pressures that tend to build up within a man while locked up for long periods of time, I worked out regularly in the prison exercise room, lifting weights, performing calisthenics, or boxing.

In addition to relieving tension, the workouts kept me physically fit, and I had a chance to witness to the others in the exercise room.

But one evening, while I was exercising alone, one of the men who used to mock me came into the room. "Preacher man," he said, "you better hurry and get back to your cell, or you're going to be in big trouble."

As I looked up at him, I noticed, for the first time, an ominous, eerie silence. No clatter, shouting or the usual

noises of early evening in the joint. "Man, what's happening?" I asked.

"The boys is starting something," he said. "Before the night is over, you gonna need that Jesus you always talking about."

That something had to be serious; I instinctively felt that a riot was about to begin. And it was imperative, when disturbances broke out, that each inmate return to his cell. Every man caught out of his cell when trouble ended could possibly be put in the hole—isolation. It also meant negative notes in a man's file, inhibiting chances for parole. I simply couldn't afford to be caught outside my cell now.

I ran back to the block in time to see an inmate grab a guard and hold him hostage. My heart started thumping double-time, and my tongue felt thick and dry in my mouth. For the leaders of the riot could, using force, drive everybody out of their cells, and otherwise well-behaved inmates would be made to participate in the riot.

Also, it makes good press for the riot leaders when the papers report that almost everyone in the block was involved, rather than just a few. In most cases, however, it is just that—a few starting the trouble. But because of threats and intimidations, others are forced to go along.

The inmate unwilling to participate in a prison riot is in a very precarious position. He dares not refuse to cooperate with the instigators; if he does, he likely faces harassment or even death at the hands of other inmates for his refusal to go along with them. And he dares not report their actions to authorities—who are unable or unwilling to protect him. Men have been killed for making reports even while in protective custody. So either way, the con loses.

All of this was racing through my mind as I heard the leaders raging through the tiers of the block. Cursing, they demanded that all cells be cleared. "Anybody caught in their cell would rather be in hell," someone shouted. There followed a banging of cell doors, loud violent swearing, fists connecting with flesh, and suddenly the lights went out.

I understood too well the law of the joint, but at the same time, I was a new Christian. How could my Christianity work in my favor if, on my record, it stated that I was involved in a riot? Somehow I had to get back to my cell, all the way up on the third tier. As I pushed for the stairs, amid the screaming and hollering and clatter, officials got on the loudspeakers and gave this terse announcement: "You have one minute to return to your cells."

The only hope I had at that moment was the Lord. "Lord," I prayed, "I know You have things for me to do in this life. But show me how I'm going to get out of this. I've got to get back to my cell."

At that moment tear gas canisters came through windows in volleys, sending stinging, pungent gas throughout the block. A panic followed, with men dashing headlong into each other, scrambling for stairs to escape the burning gas. Many passed out.

I made my move, and somehow I struggled to the third tier, hit my cell and threw my mattress against the cell door in an attempt to oust the noxious fumes. I fought for every breath of air.

The fellow in the cell next to me was also a Christian, but suffered acutely from asthma. As I placed my face in the toilet bowl, continually flushing it and hoping the rushing water would provide fresh air and relief, I could hear my neighbor cry out to the Lord for air. "God, help me. I can't stand this. I can't breathe—"

In agony, he choked for each desperate breath. Though barely able to breathe myself, I knew this man was suffering more than I, and I prayed he would be saved. In the midst of my prayer, guards broke in and began restoring order. They removed the man to the hospital where he recovered.

My next prayer was that I might be moved to B Block, the honor block, where I could be away from the more violent inmates, and where circumstances might not force me into any more compromising situations like this hastily put down riot.

By the end of the next week, I was moved to B Block.

God was really with me in this move, because a few days later, I discovered that the fellow in the next cell was also a born-again Christian.

Looking back on my prison experience, I can see where it prepared me for my ministry. There's no place where the Christian faces sterner tests than inside a penitentiary. By the same token, there's no place where the witness bears sweeter fruit.

In Stillwater, I worked nights at the powerhouse and had to sleep during the day. But right below my cell a group of inmates gambled all day on weekends, starting right after breakfast, about 7:30. During their games they'd be hollering and exhorting the dice and keeping me awake.

I not only couldn't sleep, but I was angered often when during my Bible study I'd have to hear the Lord's name abused. The old Ted Jefferson would have challenged them and would have tried to take on the whole bunch single-handed. The new Ted, reborn in the Spirit, prayed instead. "Lord, I can't love these men, but You can love them through me. You make it possible."

I went down and started witnessing to them about Christ and told them how it upset me to hear them swear. Instead of getting angry, the men accepted me. They began asking questions and we rapped for over an hour. That night one of the men came to our meeting and was saved.

Men gave their hearts to the Lord in my cell, and they'd glow with the Spirit. "Man, I just didn't know it could be like this," an older con said. "I didn't know anything could be this wonderful. I'm really free."

One day after I'd again asked for a soul in my morning prayer, no witnessing opportunities had presented themselves, and I was on my way to work. A man ran up to me and almost knocked me down the stairs. "Ted—hey, I've just got to talk to you," he said, sounding agitated and excited. "I ain't been able to sleep since you talked to me about Jesus on Tuesday. What do I have to do to accept Jesus?"

"Man," I said, smiling and gripping his hand. "You don't have to do anything or be any place special. Right here, man. Right now you can accept the Lord."

Together we prayed and that man surrendered to Christ. Truly the Holy Spirit was at work in that prison, where every week was turning into revival week.

Time was passing for me on the inside, but no longer was it dead time with counting the days until release. Now my time was productive because I was engaged in the only work that counted—the work of the Lord. But still I felt that I'd like a Christian friend from the outside to visit me—to help me along in the Spirit.

An inmate gets lonely and frustrated when he's locked up with little or no connection from the outside world. I've known guys in joints who haven't had a visit or letter from anyone outside the walls in seven or eight years. And what happens is they feel rejected and become bitter. So they reject society and determine that they are going to hurt that same society that rejected them. It's no small wonder then that maybe 7 out of 10 criminals repeat their crimes after release from jails.

Fortunately, in the Twin Cities area, there's a dedicated organization of volunteers from "straight" society interested in helping inmates. It's called Amicus, Inc. *Amicus* is the latin word for "friend," and what this wonderful group tries to accomplish is friendship. On a one-to-one basis, each member establishes a friendly relationship with an inmate inside the prison, writes to him and visits him regularly.

Ideally what happens is that when the man is released from prison, he has a straight friend to whom he can turn when he gets depressed. It's a beautiful concept, and I'm grateful for its existence, for it put me in touch with Cary Humphries.

I had written to Louise Stout, the director of Amicus, and told her that I wanted a relationship with a committed Christian friend from that organization. I told her if they couldn't find one for me right away, I'd wait.

Cary, who had long been active in trying to help out others in trouble, had discovered Amicus as a means of maybe satisfying his need to be of assistance. After reading through a few letters he came across mine. He read it and said, "I'll take this guy."

The wonderful thing about Amicus is that as inmates we know that important and sometimes influential men are members. And this gives inmates hope, because they realize that there are people on the outside who are concerned and who want to see them get a decent break after they get out.

Cary is a vice-president at Cargill, one of the largest grain dealers in the country. And yet here he was, taking time to become my friend. It was as unlikely a friendship as one could imagine—me, a black man from the slums of Milwaukee, and Cary, a southern white. Cary, well-educated, cultured, and I barely making it through grammar school.

The thing we had in common was our love for the Lord Jesus Christ, and that made up for all the other differences. We were one in the Spirit of the living God. The first time we met was in the visitor's lounge at Stillwater, and I recall the meeting as being a bit awkward at first, both of us fencing, trying to feel the other out.

"Y'all got a nice visiting room, heah," Cary said with a thick drawl that could have come straight from a Mississippi cotton patch.

"Yeah," I said, not making any commitment. Finally, Cary, not knowing what else to do, asked if I wanted to pray. And I thought, "Wow, this guy's a real Christian. Praise the Lord."

He began praying and I prayed, and we felt the Spirit of the Lord upon us. I knew the Lord was good, and the fact that two totally different dudes—a black convict from the ghetto and an important white businessman—would meet in such circumstances moved me to tears. When our prayer ended I looked at Cary, and his eyes were misty too.

If he had a single fault, it was that he wanted to do things for me. He wanted to buy different items, but I was afraid that he might think I was trying to con him, so I refused his offerings. I found out later though that he always looked in on my family while I was doing time.

Just before Christmas one year, he called Marie and asked for my children's sizes. When Christmas rolled around he was there with a load of high quality clothes and other goods. He gave my wife $50 for necessities.

But it wasn't Cary's gifts and money that made him important to his convict friend. Rather, it was knowing he'd be there when I needed him. Cary was, and is, always there.

I'm sure both Cary and I have grown spiritually from our relationship over the years, and Cary is on the board of directors of our Fair Haven Christian Household that I now operate for newly-released offenders. Cary's been instrumental in establishing this place where ex-cons can come and live and be spiritually filled as they readjust to normal society.

While in prison I used to have chances to go outside the institution to speak on prison reform, before civic and church groups. Inevitably on these visits, someone would ask me, "What made you change?"

This kind of question would give me the chance to witness for the Lord. I could say that it was His power that changed me, and nothing I could have brought on myself. I'd explain that Ted Jefferson, when left to his own devices, was a criminal through and through. But Christ made him a new person and took his old criminal desires and tendencies from him. "Only Jesus has the power to truly reform and transform a man," I'd always say.

Meanwhile, things there in Stillwater were looking up for me. I had the security of the Christians inside the joint and the support of Cary and my wife on the outside. I was much better off than most men serving time in U.S. prisons.

It was about this time, while yet serving my sentence, that I began to see the need of a Christian halfway house for ex-convicts. It was always sad to see a man return to prison when I'd watched him leaving only weeks or months before, filled with hopes and determined to make a go of it on the outside. Now he'd come back, wearing a defeated little half-smile on his face, and saying, "I guess I'm back home."

But nobody should be calling a prison home. It was especially troubling to me to see a few of our Christian brothers backslide and wind up back in prison. With tears in their eyes, they'd confess, "I just couldn't make it out there, brother. Seems like Satan himself was waiting for me."

If there's a good bit of pressure on the ordinary convict winning his release from prison, that pressure doubles when the Christian convict is let out. It needs to be fully appreciated that our prison society is an abnormal one. The environment is custodial, the essentials of life are provided and all major decisions are made for the inmates.

If a man spends three or four years in that society and then is thrust into normal society where he is suddenly on his own, where nobody rings a bell when it's time to eat or wake up or take a shower, he quickly becomes confused. Now he has to fend for himself and make decisions on his own, something he hasn't done for years.

He doesn't know how to buy a pair of shoes or what clothes are now fashionable. He doesn't see how he'll fit into a society that has changed without him. Such pressure cracks men.

The usual con simply drifts back to his old haunts and habits, because among other cons and criminals he's accepted. He has somewhere to turn, even if it only means more trouble for him.

Not so for the Christian ex-con. He can't return to his old friends because they're not of his world. But the sad fact remains that, in most cases, he can't find Christian companionship either. Too often—outside the prison— neither the Church nor society grants him acceptance. So where does he turn for help?

The Christian men in Stillwater were members of a tight, supportive group who prayed with each other, for each other and who—most importantly—loved each other. When a man from this group ventured outside, he simply would not get fed spiritually. Nor could he find fellowship.

136

The coldness of many Christian churches where strangers are ignored overwhelms the born-again ex-con now on his own for the first time. "How can Christians be so unconcerned?" he asks himself. He believes that "by their love, ye shall know them," but he finds little of this love that he can recognize...

Nobody throws an arm around him. Nobody invites him home for a family meal. He's simply left on his own by people he assumed would love him and nourish him in the Lord.

Furthermore, he doesn't understand the politics of churches, the cliques and closed circles. It is critical to his faith that he believe Christians are supposed to love Jesus and one another. But instead, our newly-released convict finds Christians bickering with each other about church matters and planning social affairs that exclude him because he's not a member. Yet neither is he asked to consider membership.

He understands loyalty to the truths of the Word of God. But he is puzzled and troubled by demands also for strict adherence to purely denominational distinctions. Too much nitpicking of this sort confuses this man who found the Lord inside the prison and who came out unaware of the many labels which believers use to pigeonhole one another.

In his confusion and rejection, the Christian ex-con finds himself alone on the outside and begins to doubt his faith. And he's almost relieved to be returned to prison where he finds acceptance once again.

If this sounds like criticism it is. There are too many professing Christians today who don't want to get their hands dirty. They retreat to their tidy suburbs and pretend that criminals, prostitutes and winos don't live nearby.

Such sterile Christians become like the Pharisee—condemned by Christ—who thanked God he was *not as other men are* (Luke 18:11). Filled with Christian pride, which may be the worst pride of all, these Christians think that in the sight of God they are better than someone else.

There's a challenge in ministering to the real down-and-out people who inhabit the underbelly of society. The work is hard. That's why it takes real Christian love and dedication—a kind of love and dedication that is in such short supply today.

Yet the rewards in lives changed and in love returned are great. And love is what Christianity is all about. Throughout the New Testament, the emphasis is on love. The potential for such love is possible in each one of us when Christ Jesus truly dwells within.

Chapter 12
RETURNING TO SOCIETY

I told him my God was alive
and would free me
from prison.

During most of my term at Stillwater I continued to suffer cleft-palate speech. And I was still ashamed to eat in public because I'd make such a mess. I had difficulty swallowing food or water and could accomplish eating only by tilting my head back and dropping the food or drink in my mouth.

My constant prayer was that I would be cured of this condition so I could preach and witness more effectively. But I'd already had four operations to repair the cleft—and none had worked.

Then after 18 months in prison, I was again sent to the University of Minnesota Hospital for more surgery. Again the operation failed. But I witnessed to my hospital roommate while I was there, and he became a Christian. So I was content, knowing that this was the reason I was hospitalized—not to be cured, but to win a soul.

Some months later, I was back in the hospital once more. And again, the operation didn't take. This time I felt frustrated and defeated and cried out, "What are you doing to me, God? I keep coming back for more pain, and things only get worse instead of better!"

Topping off this disapointment, I discovered—while still in the hospital—that I was reviewed again for parole and turned down again. While I couldn't hope for release, I still didn't take the bad news well.

While I was in the throes of my depression, a custodian

came into my hospital room one day and accidentally bumped my bed and said, "Praise the Lord."

Startled, I sat up. "What did you say?"

"Oh—uh, excuse me."

"No, you didn't say that."

Slightly embarrassed, he grinned. "Oh well, never mind. I didn't mean to run into your bed. I meant to excuse myself, but I'm a Christian, and it came out 'Praise the Lord.'"

"Hallelujah," I responded quickly, and the two of us got into an animated discussion about our Savior while he finished tidying up the room. Before he left, he told me of a young boy in another ward, a lad who had undergone numerous operations for curvature of the spine. Tomorrow, he was to have one last operation. If this one failed, the boy would remain permanently crippled.

The janitor and I prayed with the boy that afternoon and asked the Lord to guide the hands of the physicians and let the surgery succeed. When the operation took, my reason for being there was again made clear.

After a few weeks had elapsed, it was decided to give me one more chance on the surgeons' table. I went, knowing that there was a reason, even should the operation fail. But this time, the surgery was to be an unusual procedure. A sliver of bone was removed from my hip and placed in the cleft in the roof of my mouth.

It worked, and as far as I know, I'm the only man in Minneapolis who eats with his hipbone. The success of this operation gave me great joy and reason for thanksgiving, because now I was certain I would enter the Lord's ministry.

Two months later, because of good behavior and Christian witness, I was being considered for a special parole. Though the parole board was skeptical, they agreed to consider my case again.

In the foyer outside the board chambers, I sat with an inmate who followed an ethnic-oriented religion and who was also waiting for review. I told him that my God was

alive and would free me. He said his god would do the same for him.

"Only one thing," I said. "In all of your religion, you don't have a Savior. I got Somebody who's a Savior—not only for me, but for all of mankind."

As we sat there, minutes, then hours, ticked off and finally my caseworker, Judy Dorn, told me the board wouldn't make a final decision on me unto the next day. "Ted," she said earnestly, "if you've ever prayed, you pray now."

That night the inmate Christians held a prayer meeting. One of the brothers stood and said, "I believe the Lord has directed me to announce that all of us should turn toward the gate and all together pray, 'In the name of Jesus, let my brother go.' "

We obeyed, repeating over and over, "In the name of Jesus, let my brother go." All of us in those fervent minutes felt a mighty release. One of the brothers came over afterwards and draped his arm over my shoulder. His face shining, he said, "They're going to let you go,Ted. You're going to go home. Praise the Lord Jesus."

Next morning with no explanation, an official from the Commmissioner of Corrections office arrived, took a cursory look at my folder and said, "Let this man go."

The board did. The other man's special review was turned down, and my release caused some hard feelings inside the prison. He cried discrimination, claiming that I was let out because of my allegiance to a white man's God.

But everyone knew that my release was a major victory for the Christians inside, who could now openly point to the power of Almighty God. Any skeptic might now be greeted with the statement, "Well, look at Ted, man. First degree manslaughter, and he's out in 26 months. Jesus let him go. He made it and you know he wasn't supposed to get out so soon. No way, man."

But the skeptics remained doubtful, claiming that I made it because I knew some big shots on the outside.

There always will be skeptics, of course, just as there always have been skeptics, but my case was unprecedented. It's virtually unheard-of in the annals of criminal justice that a four-time loser should be released after so brief a stay for a major violent crime.

But I had been transformed. I wasn't the Ted Jefferson that had bucked the system. I was a new man, having been born again of the Spirit of our living God.

At the same time, I received a letter from authorities in Wisconsin, notifying me that they were dropping all charges against me, closing the letter by wishing me the best of luck.

My records were stamped with a special meritorious parole, which I'd earned by my Christian conduct and also by earning a second-class engineer's license and my high school equivalency. No doubt the completion of nearly a score of Bible correspondence courses also contributed.

I later discovered that over 20 people had written recommendations of merit for my special review, including the warden, whom I'd never met. Word reached him through someone on the staff who'd reported on my activities.

It was an emotional moment for me when that day of my release came in the fall of 1972. I held my last prayer session with the Christian group in prison. That original little group of five had grown and flourished during my 26 months in Stillwater until now, on the day of my departure, there were almost 40 active Christians in that little corps.

Although I was glad to be leaving, just for a moment my heart cried out for these guys whom I had learned to love as only a Christian can. They had really become my brothers in Christ Jesus. I guess they were sad, but happy for me at the same time. I told them I wouldn't forget them, that I'd be back to help them all I could.

And then as I prepared to exit through the big gate for the last time as a convict, it was a real blessing to Cary Humphries waiting for me to give me a ride home. This was the first time ever that anyone was waiting for me. What a feeling I had within as I walked through the gate. Instead of bitterness and hatred, there was joy and peace that can come only from the Lord.

What a thrill it was to be outside again, knowing my life in crime was behind me and my work for the Lord lay ahead of me. How good it was too, to be reunited with my family again and to be able to reassure them that the husband and father I ought to have been in the past, I would now become from this day forth.

Still, there were many adjustments that had to be made when I got home. I had not been the ideal father and husband. So there were lots of hurts to heal.

It's easy to say, "I forgive you," and we did that all around. But the human side of us finds it easier to say,"I forgive," than to really forgive and forget. For the heart remembers the hurts.

I'm aware of individuals who all too often say with their mouths they forgive someone, while in their hearts, they say, "But I can never forget what you did to me." No doubt there was some of this in my own family when I returned home. Trust destroyed takes time to restore.

In many ways, my return was like that of many of the POWs upon their release from Hanoi. While they had been in Viet Nam, their wives and children had gotten used to living without them. Often after the first joys of reunion, adjustments were difficult.

Marie had been in charge of our household all the time I was away, and the kids had learned to look to her for everything. So for a while, if I gave an order, they used to look at her and wonder. We had some struggles here and there, and it would have been easy for the old Ted to simply throw in the towel and quit.

I'm sure there are many new Christians who can't handle adversity. Too many of us think that once we're saved, life becomes wonderful and troubles disappear like a puff of smoke. Some of us think that, in our new joy in Christ, we can almost grow wings and fly around.

The Bible tells us we'll go through a *fiery trial* (I Peter 4:12). But we don't want to think about that. We'd rather think about verses like Matthew 11:28-30 telling us that the Lord will give us rest from our burdens. We seem to

145

think that becoming Christians means we'll live "happily ever after."

I admit that as a new Christian I too was sort of dreamy-eyed. And the problems of readjusting to a family a little bit skeptical of my sincerity were not easily overcome. But we had the Lord with us through it all, and with His help we persevered.

During the first weeks and months after my release, I found my kids starved for my love, and I was eager for theirs. And like any parent, there were times when Marie wanted to be away from the children for a while, whereas, I couldn't get enough of them. That caused a few problems between us.

I couldn't understand at the time how anyone would want to have time away from the ones he loved the most. I can certainly sympathize with Marie now, but then I wanted my whole family with me all the time. However, the passage of time and trust in Jesus brought about understanding and kept us solid.

Otherwise, like all newly-released convicts, the immediate problem facing me was to secure a job. Cary came to my aid here, lining up a position for me in the flax plant at Cargill.

Though there have been marked improvements in race relations, many white people are still uneasy about being in the presence of black folks. It's simply a matter of exposure and education. A white man who's never known a black man, or vice versa, is going to have apprehensions and misgivings.

And the foreman who was to interview me was feeling a bit nervous about it. After Cary introduced me to the man, the foreman began asking Cary how he felt I'd fit in at the plant. "Do you think he'll make it? We never had black people working with this crew before."

Cary just said, "Why don't you ask Ted?" and he left the room, leaving me alone with the foreman.

The man remained uneasy for several minutes. Finally he was able to start in with the interview, asking me about my skills and background. Cary had already told him of my ambition to be an evangelist. Perhaps that made him more comfortable. At least he could believe I wasn't going to pull a knife on him.

"Ted," he said, "you'll probably have to be a Jackie Robinson, around here for a while. Men here don't know or understand black people and things might be hard on you."

I understood. Then he said, "What's going to happen if someone calls you a 'nigger'?"

In my mind the old Ted thought, "I'll bust his head." But I found the real Ted saying, "I'm a Christian," and he accepted that.

"Say you're here, two, three years, and we have high hopes for you, and your preaching starts to interfere. What will you do?"

The answer was easy. "I'm going to serve God. I've given my life to Him. If it wasn't for Him, I wouldn't be here interviewing for this job."

As the interview wound down, I sensed the man wanted to ask me something else. He stammered around for a few seconds, then said with some embarrassment, "Ted, I hope you won't think this is stupid or get mad at me. But I've always wondered, do colored people get suntanned?"

That broke the tension and I was able to laugh. "Yeah, man," I said. "We sure do." Later in the summer I removed my watch and showed him the tan line. Another myth down the tubes!

While that incident was inoffensive and humorous, I really knew I'd changed when, two or three months after I'd begun working at the plant, a worker told a story about how black people have hard heads. He said that if engaged in a fight with one, care should be taken to hit him in the stomach because a white man would break his hand on a black man's head.

He also related a joke about a brick falling off a ladder and hitting a black man. This man guffawed and hooted, "That brick hit that nigger right in the head, and he didn't even stagger. Yup, hit that nigger right in his head."

The crew was highly embarrassed for me, but I paid no

147

attention. The storyteller had grown so used to seeing me around there, and talking to me, he no longer regarded me as a black man. I had no intention of making an incident of this, but it caused tension among the other workers.

One of them told the man that I would pipe him—lay him out—first chance I got, and the man became frightened and tried to apologize. This gave me a chance to witness to him. And after that, everyone in the yard knew I was born again, sincere in my convictions.

I worked long hours learning the work in the Cargill yard, putting in overtime and earning good money. At the same time, I preached on weekends and evenings, anywhere a congregation called. At prayer meetings, in churches, in houses, in garages.

I sensed people were moved by my testimony, for many came forward when I'd give an altar call. Doubtless this related to my background, for people could look at me and realize what God had done. They could look at themselves and reckon they'd never done anything nearly as bad as what I'd done, and if God forgave me, he'd surely forgive them.

Despite this knowledge, I began to feel a nudge of pride. People were getting saved when I spoke. Naturally I was elated, but fell into a dangerous trap that has snared many young preachers. Perhaps the public is somewhat at fault too, because when people sense a young minister has charisma, they flock around, patting him on the back.

"You saved my son!"

"You saved my husband!"

"Thank the Lord, you saved our marriage."

They give the man credit instead of God. And in my case, I half believed it. It seemed like I had forgotten the words of Jesus in John 12:32 when He said, *And I, if I be lifted up . . . will draw all men unto me.* It's so easy to glory in ourselves when we should give all the glory and honor to the Lord.

Sometime after my release from prison, I received a speaking invitation from Keith Lindberg. He and his wife used to visit me when I was still at Stillwater. Now Keith asked me to come and address a group of young people at his church in St. Paul.

There were perhaps 20 people in the gathering. And they were fine young kids, though apparently not born again. I told them what Jesus had done for me, then stopped abruptly.

"Let's stop kidding around," I said. "If you want to be sure you're going to be saved, come up here right now."

All but one of the kids came forward, and so did Keith and his pastor. Later the minister told me, "My emotions got away with me."

"Call it emotions if you want to, but that was the Holy Spirit," I said. "When those disciples left that house where they had received the Holy Spirit, people thought they were drunk. But they responded, 'No, we're not drunk like you think. It's only the third hour. We're drunk on that new wine. This is the wine of the Holy Spirit'" (author paraphrase, see Acts 2:13-15).

Incidents like this were occurring with some regularity during those early months of my ministry. While they brought new souls to the Lord, they also let pride sneak back into my heart.

I began to think that maybe I'd become a prominent evangelist with TV programs syndicated nationwide and large foundations supporting my work. I'm not knocking the vital business of evangelism, but I don't believe a true man of God should aspire to prominence for its own sake. He must be satisfied serving in whatever way the Lord wants him to serve.

Much of my non-preaching time would be spent passing out tracts on street corners downtown. And as I'd walk home on those evenings, I'd pass the Harbor Light Mission, run by the Salvation Army.

One night as I walked by, I felt a tug, as if I ought to go into the mission and talk to the people there. But I resisted that urge. Things had been going well for me. I was addressing people in nice middle-class churches. I was in demand to talk to decent, upstanding people.

I was being invited into fine homes of well-educated

149

folks, and I found these people like me. Life had never been sweeter. And in my pride, I was thinking that bums and winos were beneath my dignity. I thought I could avoid them.

But three weeks later, I went downtown again, and gave my testimony with a street corner preacher on the Nicollet Mall. It had been a fruitful afternoon, for a couple of runaways, strung out on drugs, had given their hearts to the Lord. I was on a spiritual high that night as I walked home, and again, I passed the Salvation Army.

This time I walked in and introduced myself to the brigadier. "I don't know why I'm here," I said. "But I think the Lord had directed me to this place." And I told him what had happened to me. He sat and listened, his face expressionless.

When I finished, I said, "Like I told you, I'm not sure why I'm here. Maybe I can speak to the guys in the soup line. I don't know. Maybe the Lord told you why I'm here."

As he looked at me, his face brightened. "You know what, Ted? It had to be God that sent you in here. I've been sitting here for the last hour, wondering who I could get to preach every Friday night. Do you think you could handle that?"

"Praise the Lord," I shouted. "Man, this is beautiful. These are people just like I used to be. I know they will understand where I'm coming from."

Yet it was with anxiety that I prepared my first message for that group of derelicts. It certainly would be different from the polite audiences I'd grown used to.

Now at the Salvation Army, the routine is first the message, then the soup. A couple minutes into my sermon, I began to get heckled by two men who stood up and cursed.

"Sit down, nigger. What you got to say anyway?" They kept up a constant barrage of insults, and more than once I gave thought to inviting them out into the alley to bust their heads.

But I let God submerge those feelings, and I kept on

talking. I'd gotten some advice before from the veteran mission preacher, who told me never to get into an argument. "If you argue with one," he had said, "you'll lose the whole crowd, and the devil has successfully diverted you."

So whenever they'd interrupt, I'd reply, "Talk to you later, brother. God loves you."

Sweating and emotionally drained, I finished my 30-minute message. I felt defeated but relieved too that it was over.

The men eagerly rushed toward the soup line, except for the two who'd done the heckling. They started for me. The first man reached for me, and it took a second to realize that they wanted to shake my hand. "Hey, man," he said sheepishly, "We're sorry."

During the next few minutes I was able to give them a personal witness and, as they left, another in that congregation came to me and said he wanted to know Christ.

If that wasn't reward enough, the brigadier congratulated me on the presentation. "Ted, you were made for this ministry," he said. "Very rarely have we gotten the response and comments that your preaching had tonight."

The derelict who had moments earlier been saved, shook my hand again. "Man, this is great. If God can save a guy like you, I'm in heaven, no sweat. You were one bad dude, and I come nowhere close to being that bad."

That night I knew my problems with pride were forever behind me. I knew that I could never look down on these people of the streets, the dope addicts, the alcoholics, the prostitutes, the pimps, the muggers and the rest. Inside I can hear that small, still voice of the Lord telling me that this is why I was spared, to come back to the alleys and gutters, and, like Jesus, *to seek and to save that which was lost* (Luke 19:10).

I went home that night a humble man, and all that was on my mind was "Thank you, thank you, Jesus." Because I realized that if it were not for Him, I would still be in the gutter myself.

Chapter **13**

REACHING MY OWN

Miraculously, Dad sat up and smiled.

A few weeks after my release from prison, I felt compelled to find my father. He was getting on in years now, and while I was in prison I'd heard he'd had a stroke.

As far as I knew, Dad was unsaved, and I desired to see him return to the fold. I felt responsible for him and wanted to give him my witness. But I did not know where to find him. He had moved from his old place, and somebody told me they thought he was somewhere down on the south side of town.

I spent two Saturdays looking around the neighborhoods asking about Dad, hoping for some clue regarding his whereabouts. But I came up empty-handed. He had left no forwarding address.

The second Saturday I boarded a bus at dusk and started for home. I was low and perhaps I pouted a bit, and I thought, "Well, Lord, if You don't want me to find him. I guess I won't. But if You do, Lord, then show me how to find him."

Then as the bus eased up to a stop, I happened to glance out the window again, and there was Dad, sitting at the stop, reading a paper and looking like he didn't have a care in the world. I leaped from the bus and ran to him, and we stood there hugging each other as Dad began to cry. He'd softened over the years and was truly glad to see me. We made small talk for a while, but as soon as I started to witness, he flinched and gritted his teeth. "Don't you go talking about Jesus, young Teddy."

"Dad, you're going to hell, man. You understand that, don't you? You're getting old. You've had a stroke. Man, can't you realize that I love you and want to see you saved?"

I continued seeing Dad over the next several months and our relationship blossomed. He became fond of my wife and his grandchildren but he remained hardened to the Word of God. I persisted though, and Marie and I constantly prayed for him.

Then one day, he agreed to come to my Friday night service at the mission. But when Friday arrived he didn't show. And the next week he was struck by a car, receiving serious head injuries.

He was in a coma when a friend and I came into his hospital room. We laid our hands on him and prayed for his recovery. Miraculously, Dad sat right up and smiled. He was able to be moved from intensive care to a ward and finally to a nursing home.

But his recovery was never complete. He'd lapse in and out of consciousness, and when he was conscious he was often incoherent. Doctors gave up hope.

Marie and I continued our prayers and our visitations, but nothing seemed to change. Finally Dad drifted into what doctors said was a terminal coma. "Maybe he'll last a week or 10 days," a doctor told me.

We didn't know how to continue our prayers now, for my father was lost. Finally Marie said, "Look, why don't we just pray that the Lord will give him his senses long enough for him to accept Jesus?"

The next day we went to the home and prayed. Dad had been in this coma now for two weeks, but as we prayed, he came to and started talking coherently. "It's good to see you, he said quietly.

"Dad," I said softly. "It's time, man. You're done, Dad. You better come back in, don't you think? Jesus loves you."

He gripped my hand. "I want to be saved," he said, and right there he accepted the Lord. There were tears of joy in our eyes, and as Dad's eyes filled, he said, "Young Teddy,

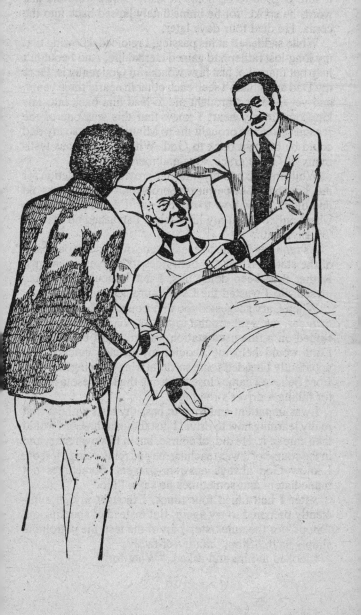

it sure is good to be home at last." Those were the last words he spoke, for he immediately lapsed back into the coma. He died four days later.

While saddened at his passing, I rejoiced, knowing that my long-lost father had gained eternal life. And I couldn't help but marvel at just how wonderful God really is. Here my Dad and I hadn't seen each other in nearly three years, and yet God had brought me to lead him back into His kingdom. In my heart I knew that this was one of the reasons God had brought me to Minneapolis—so my dad could be brought back to God. What a marvelous testimony of God's grace, love and mercy.

While my job and my ministry provided satisfaction for me, I did have one perplexing problem. I was 40 years old and didn't know how to drive a car. I'd been behind the wheel only once in my life—when I smashed up that old '32 Plymouth.

As requests for me to speak came in from various parts of the state, I'd have to bum rides to keep engagements. Rather than keep doing this, I felt I should be driving myself. So I trusted the Lord to provide me with a car.

When Cary suggested too that I ought to be having my own car, we went around to the lots on a Saturday. We settled on a fine used station wagon, and I believed the Lord would help me acquire my license quickly. But apparently I needed some spiritual wing-clipping here too. For I believe I came close to setting the Minnesota record for failing a driver's road test.

I was impatient and tried to pass my tests without first really learning how to drive. I just thought the Lord would take care of it. He did, of course, but in His own time, and in the course of it was teaching me and reinforcing a lesson. I know God always answers prayers. Sometimes not immediately and sometimes he says, "No."

After I had failed four times, I thought myself sufficiently prepared to try again. But instead of shouting out "Stop!" for the quick-stop part of the test, the patrolman simply said, "Stop," matter-of-factly.

I looked at him and asked, "What for?"

156

"Never mind," he sighed. "You've failed again."

But I made it on the sixth time, after a Christian friend spent an hour each night after work giving me instructions in a parking lot. The examiner told me after I'd finally passed, that if I had failed again, he'd have tried to keep me off state roads forever—as much for my own safety as for the safety of others.

As soon as I established my ministry in Minneapolis, my mother in Milwaukee told everyone she knew what was happening in my life. Many were skeptical because they'd known me a long time, and they knew too well the pattern of my former life. So Mom wanted me down there to show them that I'd changed.

But my ministry and job kept me tied to Minneapolis, until one night I received a long distance call from an old family acquaintance in Milwaukee. The caller was an elderly man who had known my mother many years. He was afflicted with a disease that was causing him to lose his sight. He could make out only shadowy figures. Surgery might have helped him, but he couldn't afford it.

"Ted," he said, "I believe that if you and your wife could come down here and pray for me, I just know God will heal me."

I do not believe miracles happened only in biblical times. Miracles happen every day in the name of Jesus. My conversion was a miracle—and so is the conversion of every other Christian.

I felt the request of this old friend was a signal from God that I should go to Milwaukee. So, in the midst of a howling blizzard, we left Minneapolis, driving safely through the storm to Milwaukee. I brought Ma and Marie to the man's house, and we all placed our hands upon him and asked Jesus to heal him.

And this man, after we'd prayed, removed his thick glasses. He blinked and rubbed his eyes. He smiled. He could see!

"Praise the Lord. Praise the Lord. Thank you, Jesus," was all he could say.

There was much rejoicing in his house and in the little

neighborhood church the next evening.

Several days later, the man was driving his car, and doubt began to creep in. What if his cure was only temporary and he ran into something? To prove to himself that he could gain mastery over the forces of Satan and to place full trust in the Lord, he went alone on a long fishing trip up north. He returned with his faith—and his sight—intact.

During my visit to Milwaukee, I also had the opportunity to preach in my old home church and to pass out tracts on the streets. I looked around the old neighborhood and was upset with what I saw. The same old crowd doing the same old things.

Many of my old friends had been in and out of prisons. Some had died violent deaths. Others are dead from drugs and liquor.

Garmon Harrison was one man from my past who was almost as bad a dude as I. For a time he had been married to my sister, Alice. And during our younger days, we had run the streets together.

But Garmon had since found Christ, and he was now a preacher too. What a joy it was to see him and to notice the transformation in his life, as he now led others to the knowledge of Jesus Christ.

"Man, I was bad," he said to me. "But you were worse. I didn't believe there was any way in the world you would get saved."

"Hey, I didn't *get* saved. God saved me. Jesus drew me to Him. I couldn't have gotten there myself."

"Amen," pronounced this gloriously transformed man, once criminal, now reborn in the spirit of the Lord.

But going back to Milwaukee meant experiencing personal tragedy too, for my prior life had severely damaged my relationship with my other children who still lived in Milwaukee. As much as anyone, I felt responsible for the lives they were leading—lives, for the most part, outside of God's grace. Several of the boys have been in trouble and my youngest son by my first wife is serving time in Waupun right now.

However, the Lord has enabled me to regain contact with all my children. I have spoken to each of them and, while my two oldest sons are not yet receptive, I believe the door has been opened.

I hadn't seen Kerwin, my 18-year-old son, in years, and expected real hostility from him. He hadn't forgiven me for running off and leaving him and the others. He felt that his mother wouldn't have gotten shot if I had stayed around. He carried a big chip on his shoulder for his old man.

A few years back when I first found him in Milwaukee, he was doing the same things I had done at his age. He was into pimping, pushing dope and boosting. And he was not at all delighted to become reacquainted with his long-lost daddy.

But my daughter, Jacqueline, had stayed close to my mother, and through Mom we were in touch from time to time. One day when I was visiting Mom in Milwaukee, I stopped by Jackie's place and Kerwin was there. He was hesitant about receiving me, but he hung around long enough for me to tell him I'd become a preacher. Naturally that didn't impress him and, in fact, nothing would have at that moment.

What won Kerwin over was love. After I'd received Christ, I was blessed with the capacity to love, and I told Kerwin I loved him. He probably hadn't heard anyone tell him that in a long time, and it melted him.

Still, he wasn't totally convinced. I told him I wanted him to come to Minneapolis with me. I said I'd be back in two weeks for him, if he wanted to come. He agreed to think about it.

During those two weeks, Kerwin used to drop by Jackie's place every night and tell her he didn't think I'd come for him. He used to say he really hoped I wouldn't come, and that he was better off without me. But Jackie later told me he had already packed his belongings the day after I'd come by, and he was ready to move despite what he'd tell her.

After Kerwin came back to Minneapolis with me, he received Christ, as has Jackie, and through them I feel I can reach the others in my scattered family. As things stand, they seem to be taking positive steps away from criminal activities and are no longer involved in drugs.

One of the boys, Wayne, was stoned on drugs the first time I saw him. He was not only a user, but a pusher as well. Still I gave him my testimony and prayed for him, and some months later when I saw him in Green Bay, he was not only in a halfway house, but he was a counselor there. He was free of drugs and helping others kick their habits too.

Prior to my being able to reach my children, I prayed long and hard that the Lord would give me the chance to reach them with fatherly as well as Christian love. That opportunity has been given me, and I thank God.

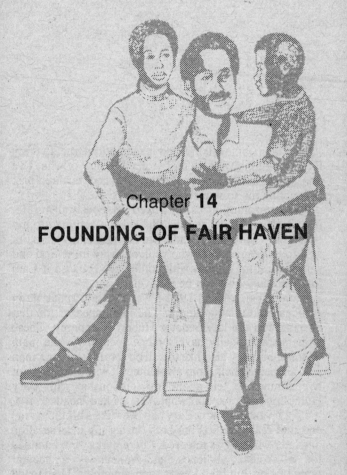

Chapter **14**

FOUNDING OF FAIR HAVEN

"What would Jesus do now?
Would He fight?"

I've had people tell me, and it's doubtless true, that my life and testimony carry more force because of what I've done and what I've been. Even my twisted, tortured past is enabling me to win souls for Christ.

Their reasoning is this: if I'd lived righteously all my life, my Christian influence might have been confined to my own family and a few friends. But because of my past, I'm able to influence many who've lived away from God and who can return to Him with confidence because if I am forgiven, they also can be forgiven.

I remember back in 1974 I was asked to speak at an Amicus fund-raising dinner. The main speaker for that evening was the late Senator Hubert Humphrey. These dinners traditionally have a name speaker for the main address, but they also like to call on a volunteer, or a man who's received help from a volunteer. I was to have about five minutes to tell about my relationship with Cary Humphries and explain what Amicus had meant to me.

I got up and told how Cary had been like a brother to me and had really helped me both during my incarceration and later when I was released. My remarks were intended for a secular audience, as Amicus is a secular organization, but I felt I had to add something. I had to tell folks that even more important than Cary Humphries, was my relationship with Jesus Christ.

So I said, "Maybe I shouldn't say this here, but the thing

that really helped me beyond all this was the fact that I became a Christian. I was never alone in my cell. Jesus' power in me enabled me to know that I could endure all things." I guess my testimony didn't last beyond a few seconds, but I sensed a stirring within the crowd.

Senator Humphrey followed me to the podium. He shook my hand and then he stood there momentarily, his eyes moist. People said later that it was one of the few moments in this great man's career that he was speechless. He said there wasn't much more he could say after what I'd said. Nevertheless, he was never one to let a chance to address an audience slip away, and he managed to give his prepared speech.

Since then, I've often been called on by Amicus to speak in its behalf, and I find this a wonderful opportunity to present what Christ has done in my life. I am also asked to speak in schools on issues like crime and penal reform. And while I'm not allowed to preach Christianity, I do say that God has played a big part in my life.

Later, when kids question me in the halls, I'm able to elaborate on my testimony. There's no doubt that kids are hungry for God's truths. Time after time I've had high school students hand me reefers and pills and say they would rather have Jesus.

And people everywhere I go can see that because of my past, knowing my desperate need to be helped and knowing that I couldn't help myself, I was able to come before the throne of grace as a child. It was easier for me to go to my knees weeping, than it is for many middle-class Christians.

For any of us—no matter who we are—to really stand up for the Lord and be of some small use to Him requires the faith of a small child. And it also requires some determination, stamina and old-fashioned guts.

I have no intellectual approach to Christ. I talk to Him the way I talk to anybody else. I fully perceive God as my Father, so I ask Him for fatherly advice and counsel. To me, prayer and communication with the heavenly Father are more than just thanking Him for blessings and asking

Him to make sick people well.

My job with Cargill was terminated in January, 1975 when I was laid off during a production lull. Though I had been praying about opening a Christian household for ex-cons, I had not been in a position to do anything about it. Yet I believed it was part of God's design for me, so instead of sulking over the layoff, I decided that perhaps now was the time I ought to get the house in operation.

Meanwhile, before my layoff, I had purchased a home for my family in a previously all-white neighborhood. This too may have been a test, for hostilities ran high. My youngsters encountered racial slurs. And one morning, I found my car covered with spit.

But my Bible tells me that if I hate a brother, I'm guilty of murder (see 1 John 3:15). So I had to help my youngest boys to learn what it means to be black—and Christian—in a white society.

After some older white boys had been particularly rough on them, they came in crying, and I overheard the eldest, who was then seven, say, "Don't bother telling Daddy about it, because he won't do anything anyway."

I put my arms around my boys and spoke with them. "You say you love me, don't you?"

"Yes, Daddy."

"What would Jesus do now? Would He fight?"

"Well, you ain't Jesus," the little fellow said.

I told them Jesus didn't fight back when they spat on Him while He carried His cross, and they agreed. "If He had struck back," I explained, "He wouldn't have been Jesus, and we wouldn't have a Savior today."

Further, I told them, "The last time I got mad, I killed a man. And if I did that again, they'd lock me up for a long time."

They understood me, and I left them with this principle: "Always ask yourself, 'What would Jesus do?' "

I believe in turning the other cheek (see Matthew 5:39). The Lord assures us that vengeance is His (see Romans 12:19). I'll do my preaching and praying, and leave the revenge to Him.

In the long run, this attitude has paid dividends. We are fully accepted in that neighborhood now, and by being accepted, we have opportunities to witness.

By early spring of 1975, I was still out of work, but a chance meeting with another man already running a local halfway house for offenders led to the establishment of the Fair Haven Christian Household. We were sitting at his table one afternoon over coffee, and he was considering accepting government funds to keep his house going. He asked what I thought, and I told him, "You let the government in, and Christ goes right out the window."

My friend agreed. "I'll trust the Lord to provide," he said, then chuckled. "Here I have a house and you don't, yet you won't take government money. Okay, I'll go with God too. And look, maybe I can help you find a house for your work too."

It just so happened that the organization he was with was in the process of buying several homes, and the next morning I went out looking at places with him. I found a house that would handle six men in a family setting. He told me the house rented for $385 a month—the exact amount in my bank account. I paid for that month and trusted the Lord to keep a cash flow coming in for the Fair Haven community. I had no staff, no plans, no idea of what to do, but I prayed that God would direct me.

Before I could open, I needed to meet certain zoning requirements. And any operations such as this would have to meet the approval of the city council. I called my alderman and informed him of my plans.

He was all for what I proposed until I told him where the house was situated. Then he said, "No way. That's all I need over in that neighborhood. I have all those street people over there already, and I don't want to add to the problem."

I turned the question back at him. "Well, where would you want me to have this house? You said you were all for it. You think this should go in an upper-class neighborhood?" I quoted Scriptures where Jesus said that a man who's well doesn't need the doctor. But the man who's sick does (see Matthew 9:12).

"This is going to be a Christian household," I said. "I don't want to tear down your neighborhood. I'm going to try and help you build it back up."

I told him about my background and what I expected to be doing. I told him what God had done for me, and how I was sure He would do the same for others in circumstances like mine, and that I thought this house was just what the neighborhood needed.

I said I knew many people in the area, because it was only a few blocks from where I took a man's life. I'd started one of the neighborhood troublemakers on pot and glue sniffing six years ago, and I said I wanted to undo some of the wrong I'd done there.

"Ted, I said 'no' at first, and I mean 'no.' But—"He paused. "Go ahead and open it up. If you have any trouble, come to me or tell them to come to me. You go there and live there and show those people what it's all about. And then when you come up for a conditional permit, I'll have some evidence to present to the council. You set an example there, and you'll have my support."

So Fair Haven opened in June 1975—but not without problems. First, I'm black, also a Christian and finally an ex-con. All these identities represent minorities. I was having drug addicts and convicts in the house, and we were living in a marginal frightened neighborhood.

One of the neighbors once told our landlord, "If you ever rent that house to a black man, I'll shoot him first and then shoot you."

But that man never threatened us. Almost from the start the power of God was at work in that neighborhood. We hadn't been in residence six weeks, when this same man's wife invited us over for dinner. There we were—blacks, an Indian and that white couple who hadn't wanted us in the place—all eating together.

Later, that man helped shovel our sidewalks in the winter, and his wife regularly brought over baked goods. They'd become part of our family and that family extended throughout the neighborhood.

There were instances, though, when houses in the area had been burglarized and suspicions first pointed toward our men. But that sort of thing has since died down. People became very suportive of us, and in our regular Tuesday evening services there are those from down the block who join us in Christian sharing.

What has happened in our neighborhood is God's handiwork for all to see. What started out to be just a household where Christian and would-be-Christian convicts, upon release from prison, could come to get rooted in Christ before moving on, has really blossomed into a full outreach ministry. Young people are coming to the Tuesday services by the busful, and folks from our fellowship are called on to give testimonies throughout the country.

One example is Vern Rollins, who was nearly killed in a shoot-out with police. A longtime lawbreaker, Vern was wanted in connection with a St. Paul holdup. So one night police staked out his house and waited for him to come home. Immediately upon his arrival, police turned on floodlights and shouted for him to surrender because he was surrounded.

But Vern was tired of life; he wanted to die, to finally be free of the misery of this life. So he whipped out his pistol and began firing. He was cut down by a barrage of police bullets and within seconds, 27 slugs riddled his body.

As Vern lay there in a pool of blood, an officer was set to finish him off. But a lieutenant stopped him. "The man's dead," he said. "There's no sense in just mutilating the body."

The ambulance was directed to take Vern to the morgue, but on the way an attendant detected movement in Vern's finger and he was rushed to the hospital. Doctors managed to save his life, though he was hospitalized off and on for several years before recovery could be called complete. There was some brain damage, however, and Vern still has difficulty remembering certain past events in his life.

When he was finally brought to Stillwater, Vern was fortunate that one of his buddies from the streets was there

168

and had become a Christian. This man witnessed to Vern and helped steer him toward God. Vern resisted and it wasn't until he was to come before the parole board that he listened seriously to the man's message.

"Vern," he said, "what do you want to get out for? You'll just kill somebody and get yourself killed. Look, you better take Jesus. At least you'll be sure of where you're going."

Later that week, Vern became a Christian at our Bible study. After his release, he often accompanied me to prisons and churches around the state where he's given forceful testimonies. There are still 13 bullets in his body, but he's alive and knows his life is a miracle. He's succeeding in his secular life too, teaching printing at a vocational high school while making moments count for his eternal reward.

Then there's young Jim Larson, my 24-year-old assistant here at Fair Haven. Jim did time for drug-related crimes, but his is an interesting case. Apparently, evidence against him was far from solid before he went on trial. But before the trial, Jim was saved, and when he appeared in court he told the judge, "All I want to do is serve my time." He pleaded guilty and was sent to Stillwater.

Since his release, Jim has been a big help to me and has also developed a marvelous facility for working with kids. He's helped organize skating parties and picnics for kids from around our area, letting them know that there's a Christian adult who wants to be their friend.

And, of course, I have to mention Ralph Johnson, who's secretary of Fair Haven. Ralph served 22 years at various penal institutions before coming to Christ. Like myself, Ralph had a fine Christian mother, but he rejected her teachings, and became something of a terror in the small Illinois town where he was raised.

Due to an illness, Ralph became bald while still in his teens and used this to his advantage as a street thug. He used to prowl the streets and pull a mugging—snatching a purse or slugging some dude and copping his wallet. He'd take off, duck around a corner, pull on a wig and go right back to his victim and help the person up. He even helped them phone police. It was quite a racket.

Ralph's a printer now and does a lot of the printing for Fair Haven, in addition to making appearance at churches and other places with our residents. He has also been instrumental in arranging for men in minimum security at Stillwater to attend our services under a guard's supervision.

One such visitor was Joe Dilworth. After a service, we sat in the front room talking about Jesus and being born again. I said, "Joe, Jesus loves you, brother, and wants you right now."

About this time I noticed the guard who was Joe's escort get up from his chair. "Man—I feel something strange here. Makes me feel all funny inside," he said.

"That's the Holy Spirit," I said softly.

"Then I want to be saved too," he said.

What a beautiful sight unfolded there as we prayed with them for salvation—two black men, an Indian, and a white guard—all joined together by the love of Jesus and one in the Spirit. The next week, Joe returned with another escort, and this guard too received the Lord.

And Joe? He's paroled now, is with us at Fair Haven and presently desires to get active in the ministry. Here's a man whose past is filled with crime and sin. But Christ changed him. We should all remember Joe's favorite verse, John 15:16. *Ye have not chosen me, but I have chosen you, and ordained you, that ye should go and bring forth fruit, and that your fruit should remain: that whatsoever ye shall ask of the Father in my name, He may give it you.*

Once, at a college conference on prison reform, I had given my testimony about how God had worked in my life and led me to reform. I told the audience that the disciples asked Jesus what the greatest commandment was, and He said, *Thou shalt love the Lord thy God with all thy heart, and with all thy soul, and with all thy mind.*

This is the first and great commandment.

And the second is like unto it, Thou shalt love thy

neighbour as thyself (Matthew 22:37-39).

A lady present said, "Well, I wouldn't mind if you were my neighbor. You're different."

"No, I'm not different," I said. "If you had known me four years ago, you'd have gone out of your way to avoid me. You say I'm all right, but if I'm getting out of prison tomorrow, and you know I'm guilty of many crimes, you might say, 'Well, I'm all for letting him out.' And then somebody says, 'But he's renting the house next, to yours.' "

The lady blanched and said, "Oh, my goodness."

"You see what I mean?" I asked. "It's all right as long as folks like us are over here—over here out of the way. The Christian community will support us and give us money. But more than that we need people to stop by and say, 'Come on, let's go have a cup of coffee.' or, 'You have any people needing work today?' "

What's too common today is for some businessman or church member to give an ex-con $50 for a new coat and then say, "See you around." Yet what the ex-con really needs even more than a new coat is another Christian's companionship and concern—especially when he's already accepted the Lord himself.

We believe *thou shalt love thy neighbor as thyself* includes every neighbor, even the ex-con. That's why we're unique here at Fair Haven—an uncommon halfway house. We feel the surest way to change a man is through the love of Christ.

Yet no parolee is forced to accept residence here. I might go so far as to say that many men coming here are not necessarily already Christians, but they are receptive to the message—or appear to be. We will accept such men.

We occasionally invite trouble by finding ourselves with men of insincere motives. We've been conned before and will no doubt be conned again. A number of inmates believe that expressing Christianity will stand them in good stead with parole board. And sometimes they're right.

Even Christians feel that a Christian can be trusted, so

171

the guy who says he's a Christian thinks he's going to look better with the board. Yet, even suspecting this motive on the part of a potential resident, we might well take him, for at the very least we're going to show him Christ in action. He's going to find Christian exposure that he wouldn't get anywhere else, and when God is ready to convict him, He will. Maybe that's tomorrow, or five years down the road. But it can happen, and because it can, we aren't likely to refuse anyone we believe can be helped.

It was in this spirit that we received a man a while back who was to become our most notorious failure. He was with us for about 30 days, then left. In the meantime, his girlfriend called one day, said she was bearing this man's child and wondered where he was. I didn't know.

Later she called to say she had miscarried. I prayed for her over the phone and later went to visit her. She became interested in our ministry and started attending our Tuesday night services. At one of these, she became converted.

She revealed she had been involved with her ex-boyfriend in a series of robberies and felt that now, as a Christian, she had to come clean. It was a dangerous thing for her to do, because at about this same time the former boyfriend, who was in the county jail, was suspected of hiring someone to commit a brutal murder. Word was out that he arranged to have somebody "hit" her too. Her testimony could prove damaging to him in court.

But she had held her ground, though she has been convicted for her part in earlier robberies. Now, while awaiting sentencing, she is teaching the children's class at our evening meetings. She has brought two of her friends with her to the meetings and both of them are also involved in teaching the children.

So even though we were burned by this former resident, because of him, three women have come to know the Lord. And we haven't given up on him either. He knows the power of God. He knows there is salvation at the Cross. He is ever in our prayers.

Chapter 15
PAYING MY DUES

"I hated you for shooting my son."

The approach of Labor Day, 1976 marked the formal end of summer. The Olympic Games in Montreal were already behind us. And the two political conventions were over, leaving Gerald Ford and Jimmy Carter to slug it out for the Presidency in November.

I listened to the same political speeches everybody else did, but there wasn't much point in my getting excited about the elections. After all, I was an ex-con— and an ex-con can have nothing to do with politics. A person convicted of a felony loses certain citizenship rights, including the right to vote and hold office. Only if a felon is discharged does he get these rights back.

When I first got out of prison in 1972, I went on parole. Then about a year later, I was granted a modified parole so I could accept preaching engagements outside the state. And I believed a modified parole was as much as I could ever expect.

There was a time, though, when my parole officer said to me, "Let me see if I can get you off parole, Ted, and get you a discharge."

And I remember thinking, "Sounds nice, but it will never happen. No way will I ever get a discharge. Not with my record. It's too farfetched." And I forgot all about it.

Then one day in early September while working at Fair Haven, I stopped by our house, picked up the mail that was lying there and took it back to work at the halfway house.

174

Not until I was back at Fair Haven did I notice one of the envelopes was from the Department of Corrections of the Minnesota Corrections Authority. More curious than anything else, I opened the envelope.

A document fell out. As I read it, I could hardly believe my eyes:

"To Theodore Jefferson, No. 24061. At a regular meeting of the Minnesota Corrections Authority, held August 27, 1976, the discharge of Theodore Jefferson, No. 24061, an inmate of the Minnesota State Prison, Stillwater, Minnesota, was authorized to take effect August 27, 1976, *and he is hereby restored to all civil rights and to full citizenship, with full right to vote and hold office, the same as if such conviction had not taken place.*" It was signed for the Minnesota Corrections Authority by R. Byrnes and Les Green.

If that document had been any longer, I wouldn't have been able to read it for the tears in my eyes. For as the meaning of the words on that simple piece of paper sank into my mind, I broke down and cried.

I wept first for shame. Even though I had not believed God for it, had not prayed for it, He had caused the authorities to grant me a full discharge. In doubting that such a thing could ever happen to me, I had forgotten that *with men it is impossible, but not with God: for with God all things are possible* (Mark 10:27). Praise God!

But I also wept for joy. My citizenship had been restored in full. Hallelujah! No longer a second-class citizen, I could now vote. And if I wanted to, I could even run for office.

For once in my life, I was completely free. No parole officer, no probation officer, no police or FBI men looking for me. *If the Son therefore shall make you free, ye shall be free indeed* (John 8:36). Thank you, Jesus!

To celebrate the occasion of my discharge, I went downtown and registered to vote. And then in November—for the first time in my life—I voted for a President, a Christian President, Jimmy Carter.

Moments of great joy are sometimes followed by

moments of great temptation. It was true of Jesus following his baptism. And it was true of me after my discharge.

Satan began whispering to me. "You're free, man, you're free. You're free to take off. Why are you hanging around here? You got a station wagon and money in the bank. So hit the road, man.

"And forget about all this faith business. It ain't nothing. It's just a way of escape. That's all it is.

But even though the devil was whispering, I wasn't listening. It was true, I was free to take off. But I was just as free to stay.

The devil doesn't call it that, but running is deserting. And for me, there would be no more running, no more deserting faith and family. Lord willing, I would stand fast, live for Him and serve Him in this prison ministry to which He had called me and upon which so many others now depended.

Since we've opened Fair Haven, the Lord has wonderfully met our need. We are providing a Christian family setting for helpless, hopeless men. And by keeping them mindful of the Lord and what He can do for them, we believe we are returning worthwhile citizens to society.

My ministry, in addition to the work at Fair Haven, includes monthly services at Stillwater and almost daily visits to the inmates as a member of the prison chaplain's staff. And I accept other outside speaking engagements whenever possible.

Being a four-time loser myself, I'm able to rap more easily with cons than perhaps someone who's always been straight. Cons have a language and life-style all their own, and when they see me and hear me, they know where I've been. But more important, they know where I am now and where I'm going. And praise the Lord, that does make an impression.

Not so long ago, we experienced a beautiful conversion there in the penitentiary. One of the black guys who really didn't appreciate our ministry used to stop in to catch the services. A militant radical, he was a tough dude within the

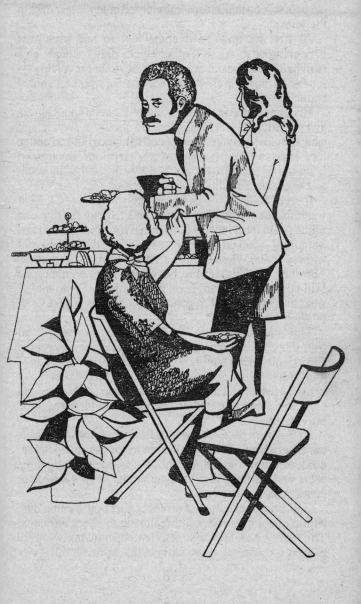

inmate society. His mere physical presence and fierce, perpetual scowl doubtless intimidated many lesser men in the joint.

At first he may have come just to see what was happening or to see to it other blacks didn't attend. This man had often spoken out in favor of violent revolution—for the killing of both whites and blacks who had gained status in society.

His attendance at these meetings did keep some blacks away, until one morning as we finished the service and sang the closing hymn, I happened to glance out and notice him. He was in his usual seat at the rear, alone. But instead of his normal dark frown, his face was directed at the pulpit and tears were rolling down his cheeks.

If ever I believed a man was unlikely to receive Christ, it was this dude. But what a joy it was to pray for him and bring him to the heavenly Kingdom. His turnabout has had a stunning effect on the prison population, though he is not without trials. When I last saw him he was not despairing. "Brother, they threaten me, but it don't scare me none," he said boldly. "The Lord is on my side now. So no matter what happens to me, I'm gonna be the winner. Praise God, brother."

This man and dozens like him in prisons and jails all over this country are in constant need of prayer. For them Christianity is not merely a privilege, it carries the sting of martyrdom in a real and chilling sense. To the best of my knowledge there have been only threats so far, but one can only pray that these threats don't result in injury to these brave men.

So the work of our fellowship flourishes, but challenges are ever present. Before we moved to our present location, a house in our old neighborhood was occupied by dope users and pushers, and the inhabitants were a source of concern to us.

One Fourth of July, the owner of that house came over with a pistol in his hands, threatening to shoot our cook. The owner was high and disoriented, thinking we were making too much noise so early in the morning. But it was

178

almost noon when he came over waving the gun in my face. "I should kill everybody in this place. I'll have 50 of my people blow you away."

I explained our situation to him, told him who we were—ex-cons like himself. He began to sympathize and inside 10 minutes, he apologized for his actions. Since then we've had other encounters with this same man, though none so serious as that first meeting. We maintain a witness to him, and he listens politely, but he continues dealing in drugs because it's more lucrative than anything else he could undertake.

But even if this man's not ready for the Lord, others of his number are. One of his people phoned me shortly before we moved to our new house and asked if he could come over and talk. I said, "Yes," and he came over—a young, white dude with shoulder-length hair and a sallow, sunken face. His eyes were ever furtive, darting. He'd obviously been strung out on drugs for some time.

When I let him in, he asked, "What kind of place is this?"

I told him we were a Christian fellowship house for former offenders. He took a deep breath. "Look, I gotta do something. I am only 25 years old, and I been in prison twice already. If things keep on going, man, I'll be back for sure. What can I do?"

"Commit your life to Jesus Christ," I said. "Let Him take your worries." I told him about my own life, how I had killed a man, yet I had been forgiven and presented with a new life—life that would be everlasting.

He stood listening to every word, then asked, "That's all there is to it?" He couldn't believe salvation is so simple. Then he glanced at his watch and, fearing reprisal from the dopers, he said he'd get back to me as soon as possible. He left quickly.

Fifteen minutes later he called. "Hey, I want that Jesus, man," he said, his voice breaking. "Old T. J. used to talk about Him and, man, there was one happy dude."

T. J. Robinson was one of our first residents here, a man truly reborn in the spirit. Last summer T. J. helped this

179

young man fix his motorcycle and, during the time they worked on the bike, T. J. maintained a constant witness to the man, planting seeds which we were able to see blossom some months later.

"All you have to do," I said, "is let the Lord come into your heart."

"I want that," he said. "Please, Jesus, help me."

We prayed together over the phone, and though he was still crying, he was deliriously happy. "I feel like a baby," he said, and he laughed.

That evening he moved out of that house, and vowed to sever all connections with his drug-associated friends. It's not going to be easy for him; pressures will mount. He won't have big money to flash and spend now. But with God's help, he'll make it.

Before he left us, he told me he'd be asking the Lord to save his old drug buddies too, and I left him with the words of Christ in John 14:27: *Peace I leave with you, my peace I give unto you: not as the world giveth, give I unto you. Let not your heart be troubled, neither let it be afraid.*

After that I noticed a few more of those men from that house watching us. The meanness seems to have gone out of them, and their attitudes have relaxed toward us. I know we left an influence on that old neighborhood.

But the move to our new place benefitted us in every way. And this is how it came about:

One day the landlord of the old place said he was going to sell the house and told us we'd have to be out by August 31, 1977. We didn't know what we were going to do, but trusted that the Lord would continue to provide. Yet late in July we still were without new lodging.

Then one night I spoke at a United Methodist church in northeast Minneapolis. Carl Johnson, a paint contractor, heard me speak there and at another engagement in Alexandria, Minnnesota. So one day he came by and said, "Ted, I don't have any money to give you, but I can give you a house. I've got a nice six-bedroom duplex you can have."

At first I thought it might be a dump that this man simply

wanted to unload as a tax write-off, but when we saw it, we knew it was the answer to our prayers. It was a fine house with a solid foundation. And it had more room, which meant our ministry could be expanded. We could look forward to taking in more men.

For our part, we'd simply assume Carl's mortgage, which meant monthly payments of only $276. Rent on the old place had risen to nearly $400.

During the weeks before and just after our move, we found how God really works through Christian people. A youth group from the Colonial Church of Edina came over one day and painted the basement. We were receiving all the furniture we needed from other churches.

And I was especially touched by a letter sent us by St. Raphael's Catholic Church. "Please do us a favor and help us," the letter began. "Tell us what you need so that we may be of service." This wasn't the condescending sort of aid offer that agencies like Fair Haven sometimes receive, but rather a sincere desire to have us help them by letting them help us.

Other calls continue to come in with various people wanting to be sure we are well provided with necessities. Praise the Lord, we are! And trusting Him, we expect to have all our additional needs met.

Meanwhile, I marvel at God's amazing grace in dealing significantly with His own. It is written that the angels in heaven rejoice when even one sinner returns to the fold (see Luke 15:7, 10). Well, no angel could have rejoiced more than I did a short time ago while speaking at Cary Humphries' suburban church. As I gave the altar call a young man came rushing forward with tears streaming down his cheeks. He was Cary Humphries, Jr.

There is no way I could ever have repaid Cary, Sr. for all he'd done for me. I'd never have his status or position, and I couldn't give him material goods. But I could give him something more precious—the knowledge that his son had come to know the Lord. It was a great moment in my life.

The other experience was one I deeply dreaded, but knew I could not avoid forever. The mother of the man I'd shot still lives in Minneapolis, and for a long while that knowledge plagued me. I feared that maybe she'd show up at a church where I was speaking and accuse me of being a hypocrite or let all her bitterness and venom out at me in front of a congregation. I wondered how I'd act, what I'd say if she started making a scene. Mostly though, I just tried putting it out of my mind.

One evening, however, I was invited to speak to a small church group where I shared the platform with the regular minister who called on me for my testimony. As usual, a number of people came up afterward to speak to me. Among these was Ethel Davis, a dear lady, who's become a mother figure to all of us connected with Fair Haven. She told me that the mother of the man I'd shot had been in the congregation that evening.

I was relieved that no scene had developed. But I still didn't know the woman, and I realized that one day soon I'd have to meet her face to face. It was a day I anticipated with real dread.

The day after this service, however, Sister Davis presented the dead man's mother with one of my recordings and asked her to listen to it. Somehow, hearing me tell what the Lord had done in my life opened the lady's heart.

Some time later both of us found ourselves as guests at a wedding reception, though again I was not aware of her presence. Had I been, I would surely have stayed away from the wedding.

I was going through the buffet line, talking and laughing with friends, when Mrs. Davis came up to me and said that the lady was not only present, but was sitting just a few feet from me. I'd have to walk past her if I wanted to get through the line, or I'd have to fight my way back through the line, stumble over people and sneak out with my wife. I thought, "No, Ted—you can't do that. You can't run from this." I prayed for courage and asked the Lord to touch that woman's heart and help both of us overcome this awkward moment.

At the same time I was hoping beyond hope that she wouldn't see me, and I could slip by her unnoticed. "So far

182

so good," I was thinking, as I helped myself to something on the table directly in front of her. I had taken a step or two beyond her and was beginning to heave a sigh of relief when I felt a tug at my sleeve. "Come here, Ted," she said. "I want to talk to you."

My heart was pounding in my throat and I sat down, sure she was going to lash out at me for killing her son. Perhaps, she'd mock my ministry. "Lord, give me strength." I prayed. "Don't let me do or say the wrong thing."

We looked at each other for an unbearable few seconds. Finally she spoke. "I used to just wait for the day I could see you and tell you how I hated you for taking my son from me," she said softly. "But you know, Ted, it's really remarkable how God can use evil for good. Remember that sign you see around, 'Prayer Changes Things'? It really does.

"You know, I saw you once in that church and, after I heard your record, I could sense that you were truly sorry in your heart for what you had done. And I know that you were glad that God was using what you had done to win others for Him."

For the first time in years, I was really free of a great burden. I had been able to forgive myself because God forgave me. And the Lord had given her enough love to forgive me for the hurt I'd brought upon her.

The two of us talked and even laughed together for the better part of an hour, and it was a real joy to fellowship with this great lady.

And what does all this mean? Simply this—that this bad dude from the Milwaukee ghetto is getting his chance to pay his dues to the Lord and is thanking Him for the chance to be in His service.

I have been miraculously saved, and every day in Christ, I'm reminded again and again that this is a beautiful, beautiful life. Jesus has given me eternal life and I don't have to wait until I get to heaven to enjoy it. I'm living it right now. And that's a fact.

My body may die some day, but I'm going to live

forever. I know it because Jesus is alive right now and living His life in me. I know Christ is in me.

The Apostle Paul said it best: *I am crucified with Christ: nevertheless I live; yet not I, but Christ liveth in me: and the life which I now live in the flesh I live by the faith of the Son of God, who loved me, and gave himself for me* (Galatians 2:20).

Yes, God in Christ in you. Jesus is in each one who worships in His name. And when we believe that, we can really begin to live life—live life more abundantly—no matter what our ages might be (see John 10:10). And what a blessing that life can be!

If enough people everywhere truly believed that Jesus is alive right now, and lived as though they believed it, we'd see a world change overnight. Because both the world and change begin with each one of us.

Ted Jefferson

The mailing address of Mr. Jefferson is:

Ted Jefferson
Fairhaven
Box 11056
Minneapolis, Minnesota 55411